ASSESSING SPIRITUAL NEEDS

ASSESSING SPIRITUAL NEEDS

A GUIDE FOR CAREGIVERS

Academic
RENEWAL PRESS
www.arpress.com

To Judy, with love and gratitude

ASSESSING SPIRITUAL NEEDS
A Guide for Caregivers

REVISED EDITION 2002

First Academic Renewal Press Edition 2002
Copyright © 2002 by
Academic Renewal Press

Scripture quotations are from the *New Revised Standard Version Bible*, copyright © 1989 by the Division of Christian Education of the National Council of the Churches of Christ in the United States of America. Used with permission.

Excerpts from *Pocket Guide to Nursing Diagnoses*, third ed., by Mi Ja Kim, Gertrude K. McFarland, and Audrey McLane (St. Louis: The C. V. Mosby Co., 1989). Used by permission of the author.

Excerpts from *Nursing Diagnosis: Application to Clinical Practice* by Lynda Juall Carpenito (Philadelphia: J. B. Lippincott Co., 1983). Used by permission of the author.

Library Of Congress Cataloging In Publication Data pending

ISBN 0-7880-9940-X   PRINTED IN U.S.A.

CONTENTS

PREFACE

Why should you be interested in spiritual assessment? My interest in this topic has always been sparked by a specific practical need or question that called for my response. My guess is that your interest in spiritual assessment has the same source, the need to clarify the way in which your ministry takes into account and responds to the spiritual dimension of life.

Over the past twenty years I have made several attempts to understand spiritual assessment. Each time, the specific questions I pondered and the resources I had available were different. In 1971, during my pastoral care residency, I was assigned to the hospital's psychiatric units. One of the issues I struggled with was discerning the difference between my identity and work in that setting and those of my colleagues in social work and psychiatry. The resources I consulted then were Edgar Draper's *Psychiatry and Pastoral Care*, The American Psychiatric Association's DSM-II, and Paul Tillich's concept of faith as ultimate concern.[1] I did my best to summarize my ideas in a didactic presentation to my peers on pastoral diagnosis.

Fifteen years later I found myself trying to find the best way to teach pastoral care to our CPE (Clinical Pastoral Education) students. As a supervisor I had guidelines that informed my evaluation of a student's ministry. Could I make those guidelines explicit and teach them to my students? Again I looked for resources. I was impressed by the work that was developing in nursing diagnosis and by the APA's new DSM-III.[2] I also discovered the important work that had been done by Paul Pruyser on spiritual diagnosis and by James Fowler on faith development.[3]

Several years later, when a colleague on our nursing faculty sought information on models of spiritual assessment that nurses could use in their initial patient evaluations, a team of four of us began several years of collaboration on the topic. During that time we reviewed many of the models for spiritual assessment that were available, developed some ideas for evaluating the strengths and weaknesses of different models, and even tried our hand at developing a model of our own. A great deal of what I have to share in this book comes from the work we did together at that time.

In the past twenty years much has happened in the area of spiritual assessment. A lot of interesting work is going on right now. It isn't possible to write a definitive text on such a dynamic subject. It is possible to write a workbook, to summarize where we are, to review the resources we have available, and to invite you to make your own contribution to the development of this subject.

This book is intended for pastoral practitioners in various settings, congregational leaders, institutional chaplains, and pastoral counselors, as well as those in related helping professions. I hope that readers will test what I have written against what they are doing, what they find effective and ineffective in their approaches to spiritual assessment. I would like to know what readers think about all this and to find out what more we can learn from one another.

In chapter 1 I begin with a description of where we are in spiritual assessment in pastoral ministry, describe recent developments in the field, define the concept of spiritual assessment, discuss why spiritual assessment is important, and offer a brief theology for spiritual assessment. In chapter 2 I present a case to illustrate more specifically the way spiritual assessment contributes to pastoral ministry. In chapter 3 I describe the concepts behind the spiritual assessment model used in chapter 2. Chapters 4 and 5 apply that model to two more cases. In chapter 6 I describe a set of guidelines for evaluating the strengths and weaknesses of various models of spiritual assessment. In chapter 7 I evaluate three popular models of spiritual assessment using those guidelines. Chapter 8 concludes the book with a discussion of the spirit and the person doing spiritual assessment and some directions for further work in this area.

I want to express my gratitude to the many people who have been part of the development of this book and the ideas in it. I am grateful to the patients and parishioners who have allowed my students, my colleagues, and me to share a portion of their struggles with them, especially the three whose cases are presented here. Their openness and trust provided the need and opportunity to develop these ideas about spiritual assessment.

My colleagues Julia Quiring Emblen, Carol J. Farran, and J. Russell Burck played an important role in developing key ideas in this book. We worked together for almost two years reviewing the literature in the field and developing the model of spiritual assessment presented in chapter 3. Our work together provided me with a level of professional stimulation, discipline, and critical feedback I had never before experienced. It was an exciting process, and it gives me pleasure to acknowledge the significant contribution that they made to the ideas presented here.

The first drafts of some of this material were written in the summer of 1987. Professor James Ashbrook of Garrett-Evangelical Theological Seminary in Evanston, Illinois, provided me with a quiet place to do that writing. I am grateful for the support and hospitality that he and his colleagues offered to me that summer.

Over the past five years I have presented earlier versions of some of this material at various conferences. I want to express my gratitude to colleagues who heard those presentations and offered their encouragement and critique. I particularly want to acknowledge my appreciation for the support and critical response of Don Browning, Roger Fallot, and Michael Donohue, each of whom was a formal respondent to one portion of this project or another at an earlier presentation. As I began more research in this field, I learned that Steven Ivy was also working in the area of spiritual assessment. It has been a pleasure to get to know Steve and to benefit from his knowledge and critical discussion of this subject. I am grateful for the support he has offered me in this work. I had some difficulty as I began the actual writing of this book. I am grateful to my friend and colleague Herbert Anderson for his encouragement and for some very helpful suggestions he made about the outline.

I would not have been able to pursue my interests in this topic without the strong support of my department chairs, first Chris Hovde and more recently Larry Burton. The encouragement and challenges of my departmental colleagues and students have also helped me stay with this work at important times. I am especially grateful for permission to include two cases in the book by former students MaryJo DiDomenico and Deb Reed. The spiritual assessment of the case of Bob in chapter 5 was first discussed in an AIDS spiritual assessment research team meeting. I want to thank team members Jim Corrigan, MaryJo DiDomenico, Carol Reese, Deb Reed, Ed Stivers, and Ray Sousa, who contributed to the initial spiritual assessment of that case, and also Ken Crossman, research assistant for that project, who wrote the first draft of that assessment.

I also wish to thank my colleagues Bill Gilmer and Larry Burton and my students Jim Stern, Espiridion Elizondo, and Jeff Grumley, who read one or more of the chapters and offered helpful advice. I am especially grateful to my students Tom Coffey, Kirsten Peachey, and Fletcher Harper, who read and discussed the whole manuscript with me. My editors, Joan Hemenway, representing the College of Chaplains, and Irene Getz, from Augsburg Fortress, offered many suggestions that helped improve the book. I thank them for their generous assistance.

Finally I want to express my appreciation to my wife, Judy. She was the first reader for many of these chapters and provided just the right mix of critique and support. I also wish to express my deep appreciation to Judy and my daughters, Sarah and Rebekah, for their understanding and support while I was working on this project.

NOTES

1. Edgar Draper, *Psychiatry and Pastoral Care* (Englewood Cliffs, N.J.: Prentice-Hall, 1965); American Psychiatric Association, *Diagnostic and Statistical Manual of Mental Disorders*, 2d ed. (Washington, D.C., APA, 1968); and Paul Tillich, *The Dynamics of Faith* (New York: Harper & Row, 1957).

2. Mi Ja Kim and Derry Ann Moritz, eds. *Classification of Nursing Diagnoses: Proceedings of the Third and Fourth National Conferences* (New York: McGraw-Hill, 1982), and American Psychiatric Association, *Diagnostic and Statistical Manual of Mental Disorders*, 3d ed. (Washington, D.C.: APA, 1980).

3. Paul Pruyser, *The Minister as Diagnostician* (Philadelphia: Westminster Press, 1976); James W. Fowler, *Stages of Faith* (San Francisco: Harper & Row, 1981).

Chapter 1

THE PLACE OF ASSESSMENT IN PASTORAL CARE

Cornelius is a retired tool and die maker in his early seventies who has had Parkinson's disease for over a dozen years.[1] Cornelius has been married for many years and has two sons of whom he is very proud. Much of the pleasure Cornelius finds in life comes from his visits with his sons, their wives, and his grandchildren. His Parkinson's has gotten worse in recent years, but medication has provided some control. Recently his neurologist admitted him to the hospital to see if some adjustment in his medication would improve his symptoms. One night during this hospitalization Cornelius had a frightening dream. In his dream he saw snakes behaving in threatening and lewd ways. He also saw one person being shot by another person with a pistol. He woke from his sleep anxious and afraid and called for the nurse.

Do you think this is a situation where a pastor or chaplain should be called? Later that morning I received a request from Cornelius's nurse to visit him. She had talked with Cornelius and his wife about his dream and had asked if they would like her to call a chaplain. They told the nurse it would be all right if she contacted the chaplain. When I arrived, I visited with Cornelius and asked him to share with me what had happened. I also talked with his wife, nurse, and physician to learn more about the situation and what, if anything, I could do to help.

How did the nurse or Cornelius or his wife decide that this was a situation in which a religious counselor should be called? What guidelines could inform me as I tried to understand if this was a case where my pastoral ministry was needed? What goals should shape my ministry, and how would I know if my efforts had helped achieve those goals?

Pastors of congregations, institutional chaplains, and other pastoral practitioners look for ways to find answers to these questions. Doing so requires a process called spiritual assessment, an assessment that focuses on the spiritual aspect of life. As a way to begin this discussion of spiritual assessment, I want to review four areas that will provide background for the later chapters. The four areas are the current state of spiritual assessment in pastoral ministry, the meaning of spiritual assessment, its significance, and a brief theology for spiritual assessment.

Spiritual Assessment in Current
Pastoral Care

A few years ago one of my colleagues asked several hospital chaplains to describe their approaches to spiritual assessment.[2] Their responses revealed a great diversity in understanding and approach. For a few the question was puzzling. They didn't know what assessment meant. They weren't aware of making assessments in their work. They simply followed institutional protocols and offered pastoral care to all patients and families. In contrast to this, one of the chaplains used a set of forms to guide patients through a self-assessment of faith using a model from Paul Pruyser.[3] He not only used an explicit method for spiritual assessment, he also had developed a set of guidelines for when he would use this assessment tool and when he would not.

The chaplains in the survey were asked to describe how and when they made spiritual assessments. The approaches to spiritual assessment they described included a friendly greeting, "How are you today?"; a Rogerian, nondirective approach; and a direct approach, "I let them know who I am, what I represent, and inquire how they think I can be of help." There was a similar diversity when the chaplains were asked at what point they made a spiritual assessment. Some said, "Not at the first visit"; others said, "Constantly." One chaplain replied that he made an initial assessment "rapidly" to see whether to continue the visit.

The chaplains were also asked to describe the most common spiritual needs they encountered. Their responses included dynamic needs, some of which were explicitly religious (sinfulness, grace, revelation, reconciliation) and some more psychosocial (alienation, loneliness, depression, hostility). Sacramental and ritual needs such as anointing or communion were mentioned. The need for a relationship with the pastor was also described.[4]

This brief study revealed that some assessment takes place in pastoral care, but it is marked by considerable inconsistency. I have identified nine characteristic features of approaches to spiritual assessment.

1. *Implicit Assessment.* This is one of the most common forms of assessment in pastoral care. We usually do not think of such assessments as assessment, and consequently they are never shared with the person who is the object of our care nor with any other concerned or interested person. But observing the differences in how we relate to different persons as we offer pastoral ministry, we can infer that some process of assessment has implicitly taken place.

2. *Inspired Assessment.* Inspired pastoral actions are grounded in divine revelation received directly by the caregiver or mediated through holy texts or persons. An example of this approach to assessment is when we refer to the biblical instruction to the sick to call for the elders to come and pray and anoint with oil. It is also reflected in the pastor who reports, "I didn't know

what I should say next, so I closed my eyes and prayed for guidance and then it came to me that I should. . . ." The actions or instructions of teachers or mentors whom we regard as inspired can also provide guidance for our pastoral actions.

3. *Intuitive Assessment.* Pastoral caregivers frequently say that their ministry with a specific parishioner or patient was directed by intuition. Some describe their intuitions as feelings or sensations, "I just had this gut feeling. . . ." Others report that what they call intuition may be the very rapid gathering of verbal and nonverbal information. In these cases our perceptions are taken in so quickly, observing so many things about the situation, person, and environment simultaneously, that we aren't able to remember looking for specific things. We just find ourselves with a conviction about what is needed in this case and are at a loss to explain how we came to this conviction.

4. *Idiosyncratic Assessment.* This differs from implicit assessment by being regarded by the caregiver as an assessment. But these assessments are derived from the unique person, knowledge, or gifts of the caregiver. When we make idiosyncratic assessments, we do not share them with others, we usually have no set of criteria to guide our process, no explicit method, no testing of our approach, and no common language or viewpoint shared with others in the field. As chaplain Clark Aist says, "Each of us probably has an ad hoc diagnostic schema of our own."[5]

Another type of idiosyncratic assessment is seen in pastors and caregivers who have no rationale for the directions their ministry takes. For some the question of why we do what we do violates our trust in ourselves and whatever spontaneously emerges in any situation. For others the question is simply confusing, and we just can't answer it.

5. *Assessments Based on Traditional Pastoral Acts.* I think a considerable portion, perhaps a majority, of our pastoral assessments are best described under the category of pastoral actions that are traditionally expected in the context of a specific life situation. The specific pastoral action may vary from tradition to tradition, but within the tradition there is a strong consensus about what should be done. For instance, when a Roman Catholic family hears the news that a loved one is near death, they call the priest, who immediately comes to administer last rites.

Russell Dicks, an important leader in the field of pastoral care earlier in this century, described the expectations regarding the use of prayer in the Protestant tradition. "The most frequent occasions when the pastor will pray orally in pastoral calling and counseling will be: in routine calling; when calling upon the sick; in ministering to the dying; with the bereaved; and calling upon older people. Only occasionally will [the pastor] offer a prayer in formal counseling."[6]

A more modern version of this approach to assessment is found in the following recommendations for ministry to bereaved men. "The pastor should help the individual to accept the pain of bereavement. . . . Men, especially, try to avoid showing emotion, as some think it is a sign of weakness. The pastor should encourage the expression of grief where there are signs that the individual is fighting against it. This encouragement can be given through a gentle suggestion as, 'Go ahead and cry. I would do the same, if I were in your place.' "[7]

Some pastoral actions are upheld by the norms of an institution as well as a faith group. Certain hospitals, for example, routinely offer a pastoral visit and prayer (Protestant) or the Sacrament of the Sick (Roman Catholic) for all patients on the surgery schedule. The expected ministry may vary, but certain life situations predictably provide us with cues for our pastoral action.

6. *Assessment Based on Normative Pastoral Stances.* For some of us the approach to assessment focuses on our attitude or stance rather than on our behavior or on the explicit need of the patient. We believe that what is important is for the pastor to "be present," to "be available," to "be empathic," to "be authentic," or to "offer hospitality." The specific behavior performed is less important here than the overall stance or quality of our relationship with the person we're caring for.

7. *Global Assessments.* Another common approach to pastoral assessments is to employ one or two very broad diagnostic categories. For example, we may believe it is important to be cheerful and encouraging when we make hospital calls in order to counteract the loneliness and anxiety that anyone who is sick and in the hospital is feeling.

8. *Psychological Assessment.* When psychologist Paul Pruyser reviewed the situation in spiritual assessment, he was dismayed not by the implicit or idiosyncratic features of the assessments but by the perception "that clinically trained pastors, if they think diagnostically at all, typically do so by using psychiatric categories and psychiatric language."[8] I find it hard to argue with Pruyser's observation about the significant role psychological assessments play in our work. Yet I don't share all of his dismay about this fact.

9. *Explicit Spiritual Assessment.* Sometimes our pastoral care is based on a conscious process of spiritual assessment of what the person needs or what the situation calls for. Later in this book we will review some of the models that are more widely used for explicit spiritual assessment.

From this review of approaches to spiritual assessment we can see that probably only a small portion of the pastoral care we offer is guided by a conscious assessment of spiritual need. This is not surprising when we consider how pastoral caregivers have been taught pastoral care in recent years.

The focus of teaching and training in pastoral care has been in four areas: the sharing of relevant knowledge from the behavioral sciences, particularly dynamic psychology; the attainment of counseling skills; the integration or correlation of psychology, counseling, and the behavioral sciences with theology; and the development of the self and identity of the pastoral caregiver.

In none of these areas has assessment been a major focus. In fact, as Pruyser observes, the strong influence of the work of Carl Rogers on pastoral care led to a bias against diagnosis in pastoral care.

> This school explicitly scorns any division, in time, or principle, between diagnosis and treatment, and goes on to find prior assessment and diagnosis distasteful for several reasons. At its best, it holds that the counseling process is designed to let the counselee discover for [herself or] himself what [her or] his problems are, with the clarifying help of the counselor. . . . At its worst, Rogerian theory and practice find diagnosis offensive, originally because of an alleged authoritarianism that it found inherent in all diagnosing.[9]

Practical training in pastoral care has done little to change this. Clinical Pastoral Education (CPE), for example, has placed emphasis on two of the four areas noted above: growth in the pastor's self-understanding, including the ability to enter into empathic, growth-producing relations with others; and basic listening and counseling skills. This focus, coupled with a predominantly case-based, experiential approach to learning, has thereby deemphasized the teaching of assessment in pastoral care, thus diminishing its role in guiding pastoral actions.

The situation has been changing, however. In recent years there has been a striking increase of interest in spiritual assessment. What has caused this change? In hospital-based ministry, one cause is the institutional demand for accountability. Another cause is the maturing of the field of pastoral psychotherapy, where attention is shifting from mastery of psychological skills and knowledge to the integration of distinct theological perspectives. In parish-based ministries, as in specialized ministries, there may also be greater awareness of the distinctiveness of spiritual care and a desire to be more explicit in providing it.

Interest in spiritual assessment has also been fueled by work published in the last twenty years. In *The Minister as Diagnostician*, Paul Pruyser strongly stated the need for pastors to be attentive to the diagnostic aspect of their work. He urged that this process be shaped not by the borrowed perspective of psychology but by the pastor's distinctive theological perspective. Pruyser suggested a set of guidelines for pastoral diagnosis and provided some examples, applying those guidelines to pastoral care. Pruyser's central argument was very persuasive, and the increased interest in assessment in pastoral care in recent years testifies to that. I will discuss Pruyser's work further in chapter 7.

One of the issues that challenges modern pastoral care and counseling, and by extension assessment in pastoral care, is that of authority. "To what degree should [the pastoral] relationship involve the authority of the [guide] over the [guided person]?"[10] Don Browning has addressed this question in his writing, arguing that we cannot and should not strive toward value neutrality in pastoral care. In fact Browning proposes that the process of diagnosis in pastoral care must address both what is (the descriptive) and what ought to be (the normative). "The full task of assessment and diagnosis," he writes, "involves answering both questions."[11]

In the last twenty years a significant shift has occurred regarding the issues of language and authority in ministry.[12] Pruyser's and Browning's work reflects that shift, which has had a major impact on pastors and other religious caregivers and on our work with spiritual assessment. Fifteen or twenty years ago, the "death of God" theology expressed the perception that religious language was no longer meaningful for many people. One author of the time, Sam Keen, wrote that the "myths of religion are no longer supported by any authority strong enough to command the respect of an unprejudiced inquirer. . . . For the moment, at least, we must put all orthodox stories in brackets and suspend whatever remains of our belief-ful attitudes."[13] Such a judgment is at odds with the perception that now informs Pruyser, Browning, and the renewed interest in spiritual assessment we are observing.

To summarize so far, I have offered an overview of the place of spiritual assessment in pastoral care, indicating that for the most part it has not received much attention. I have also described some recent work, both theoretical and clinical, indicating a growth of interest in spiritual assessment. Next I will define spiritual assessment and describe its importance for pastoral care.

Spiritual Assessment: What Is It?

What do I mean by spiritual assessment? Both terms in the phrase need to be defined.

I define the spiritual as the dimension of life that reflects the need to find meaning in existence and in which we respond to the sacred.[14] In this work I don't make distinctions between the term *spiritual* and the related terms: *spirituality, religion, religiosity, pastoral, faith,* or *belief.* In fact I use the terms interchangeably at times. In doing so I am not unaware of the sometimes helpful and important distinctions in these terms,[15] however, for our purposes here the distinctions are not important. In chapter 6 I will offer a further discussion of various approaches to defining the spiritual dimension of life and their significance for spiritual assessment.

I also don't make distinctions between the terms *assessment* and *diagnosis.* I sometimes use the terms interchangeably. Other professions often reserve the term *diagnosis* for the label or name given to a disease and use *assessment* for the information gathering and interpreting process that leads to the diagnosis. I prefer the common usage in which the terms are essentially identical. In reviewing the original meaning of the Greek roots of the words diagnosis and to diagnose, Pruyser writes, "They are used to mean discerning and discriminating in any field of knowledge, distinguishing one condition from another, and, by derivation, resolving or deciding. . . . To diagnose means grasping things as they really are, so as to do the right thing."[16] It also results in tapping into common and agreed-upon knowledge in a given field in order to be more effective. In this context Pruyser notes what may be obvious— that is, that this discerning process has never been the sole prerogative of medicine.

Assessment is both a statement of a perception and a process of information gathering and interpreting. I use the term *assessment* as a noun and a verb. Because it is both process and content, it is inherently a dynamic concept.

The assessment process contains both objective and interpretive aspects. A nurse's assessment may, for example, describe "spiritual distress related to inability to practice spiritual rituals." Her objective data includes "Requests spiritual articles, reading materials, sacraments . . ." and "is unable to maintain usual contact with spiritual leader."[17] In evaluating whether spiritual distress is present, the nurse must also make some interpretations, determining if the patient "is discouraged" or "has ambivalent feelings (doubts) about beliefs" or "feels a sense of spiritual emptiness" among other things.[18]

Assessments also have both descriptive and normative aspects. The American Psychiatric Association's Diagnostic and Statistical Manual (DSM-IIIR) for mental illness illustrates both aspects. The manual attempts to offer a comprehensive description of the signs of various mental disorders. "DSM-IIIR can be said to be 'descriptive' in that the definitions of the disorders are generally limited to descriptions of the clinical features of the disorders. The characteristic features consist of easily identifiable behavioral signs or symptoms, such as disorientation, mood disturbance, or psychomotor agitation, which require a minimal amount of inference on the part of the observer."[19]

The descriptive aspects of the diagnosis are most obvious in the diagnoses made on what is called Axis I, the clinical syndromes. For a major depressive episode, for instance, these are some of the diagnostic criteria:

A. At least five of the following symptoms have been present during the same two-week period and represent a change from previous functioning; at least one of the symptoms is either (1) depressed mood or (2) loss of interest or pleasure.

   (1) depressed mood . . . most of the day, nearly every day, as indicated either by subjective account or observation by others

   (2) marked diminished interest or pleasure in all, or almost all, activities most of the day, nearly every day (as indicated either by subjective account or observation by others of apathy most of the time)

   (3) significant weight loss or weight gain when not dieting (e.g., more than 5% of body weight in a month), or decrease or increase in appetite nearly every day

   (4) insomnia or hypersomnia nearly every day

(5) psychomotor agitation or retardation nearly every day (observable by others, not merely subjective feelings of restlessness or being slowed down)

(6) fatigue or loss of energy nearly every day

(7) feelings of worthlessness or excessive or inappropriate guilt (which may be delusional) nearly every day (not merely self-reproach or guilt about being sick)

(8) diminished ability to think or concentrate, or indecisiveness, nearly every day (either by subjective account or as observed by others)

(9) recurrent thoughts of death (not just fear of dying), recurrent suicidal ideation without a specific plan, or a suicide attempt or a specific plan for committing suicide. [20]

The normative aspects of diagnosis are most obvious in the Axis V diagnosis, where the clinician indicates his or her judgment of an individual's current level of functioning or highest level of functioning during the past year. [21]

Are there any limits to what we can assess? It's hard to think of them. We make assessments of living and nonliving things. We make assessments of small things (molecules and cells) and large things (elephants and whales). We make assessments of ourselves, of others, and of relationships, ones we're part of and ones we're outside. Assessments can focus on things, people, neighborhoods, states, nations, our whole planet. Assessments can focus on the past (what was Martin Luther's personality type?), the present (to whom do you turn for emotional support?), or the future, a prognosis (how soon do you plan to return to work?).

In the clinical context a care plan is often based on a complex of different assessments, of the person who comes for help, of myself as potential helper, of the context in which the help might take place, and of the other resources available. Such complex, multifocused assessments are often guided by questions such as, What does this person want? What do I think he needs? Do I feel qualified to help him? Do I have the time in my schedule? Am I favorably disposed toward trying to help him? What kind of help is expected or required of me in the institutional context of this assessment (compare the patient's hospital room and the parish pastor's office)? What are the likely consequences if I elect to do more or to do less than is expected? What other departments or services will also be involved in the patient's or family's care? What additional resources will be needed to help this person or to help me help him? Are those resources available? If not, is it better to postpone any intervention until they are?

When is the best time to make an assessment? As I noted earlier, one of the chaplains in our survey was careful not to make an assessment until he had gotten to know a patient, during a second visit at the earliest. Yet one of his colleagues candidly noted that he began to size up the situation as soon as he walked into the patient's room, "Am I welcome here today or not?"

Some situations lend themselves to adequate assessment at one point in time. Reevaluation at sequential points in time, however, is frequently helpful or normative. In medicine, for example, the patient has an admitting diagnosis, a subsequently confirmed or revised diagnosis that guides the therapy, a discharge diagnosis, and in some cases a diagnosis based on a postmortem examination.

In other situations, observations of changes or their absence over time constitutes a specific diagnostic criterion. In DSM-IIIR, for example "the diagnosis of Schizophrenia requires that continuous signs of the illness have been present for at least six months."[22] In the psychoanalytic treatment of narcissistic personality or behavior disorders, according to Heinz Kohut, it is necessary to wait to see if one of the characteristic narcissistic transferences develops before one makes a definitive diagnosis.[23]

What then is the relation between assessment and treatment? It appears self-evident that they are sequential, that treatment doesn't begin until assessment is concluded. But things are not in fact that clear. In medical cases, colds, for example, the failure of one therapeutic approach often provides the basis for an alternative assessment and course of therapy. We sometimes have a similar approach to household or auto repairs: When a very thorough assessment seems too forbidding, we try a simple remedy first. Its success or failure then helps us to make a more definitive assessment and to decide if further repairs are needed.

But in addition to these ways in which therapy helps establish an assessment, the process of assessment is often therapeutic in and of itself. The empathic interest of another person in our distress can do much to reduce distress or at least take the edge off it. Having an expert provide us with a name for a condition that hurts and frightens us can provide relief from nightmares when we fear the worst or fear that our condition is without name or remedy.

Yet diagnosis is not something only a professional is qualified to perform. We actually do a considerable amount of self-diagnosis. "This engine is making an awful sound. I wonder if it needs a tune-up?" "I've had this cold for over a week. Maybe I ought to call the doctor." A person who decides to consult a professional, Paul Pruyser points out, has already done a certain amount of self-diagnosis. "The person seeking help is already on the road toward articulating some understanding of himself," states Pruyser. "He is already taking stock of himself, he has already begun to diagnose himself by seeking some prospective helper. In selecting one kind of helper rather than another he is already channeling the diagnostic process in a certain direction."[24]

There are some assessments, whether the car's problem is the alternator or the generator, for example, that few of us can make for ourselves. Most of us will depend on specially trained helpers who have access to the knowledge and the technology required to make proper assessments. Other assessments not only require special knowledge and diagnostic equipment, but can be made only by persons with a special license to do so. Only a licensed physician, for example, can make a diagnosis that qualifies a person to receive disability insurance.

In summary, I have indicated here the many ways in which the term *assessment* is used and many situations to which it can refer. We have seen that assessments can at times be simple and at other times complex. All of the meanings of *assessment* that I have reviewed here have a place in the assessment of the spiritual dimension of life. Now I want to discuss why spiritual assessment is important.

The Importance of Spiritual Assessment

Spiritual assessment has a central place in guiding and evaluating pastoral care. I will discuss the importance of spiritual assessment by examining the foundation it provides for action, communication, contracting, evaluation, accountability, quality assurance, and research. I will also discuss the role of assessment in defining a profession.

1. A Foundation for Action. One of the chief reasons for giving our time and attention to the process of spiritual assessment is that assessments guide our efforts to help another; they help us set goals for our ministry. The alternative to assessment-guided ministry is spontaneous or impulsive care. Assessment-guided, goal-directed pastoral care is more likely than spontaneous care to have the desired or agreed upon effect and less likely to make matters worse.

2. A Foundation for Communication. Related to action and frequently preceding it is communication, conversation about whether a person thinks there is a problem here and whether or not I agree with him or her. Or, if we agree a problem exists, how do we describe it? The work of assessment directs our attention and thus also our communication to central matters of observation, data, interpretation, and our understanding of their implications for our actions. My assessment is aided as I talk it over with the person and find points of agreement. It is helped even when we have points of disagreement, because this compels us to take another look at the data. It is in the process of assessment as communication that the person seeking help and the counselor can arrive together at the clearest possible description of the situation.

3. A Foundation for Contracting. To have a plan of action requires that we have an agreement, a contract or covenant, about who will do what and when, about why we are undertaking this plan and what outcome or changes we expect. The assessment process allows the person seeking help and the caregiver to develop such a contract. It also provides a basis for enlisting the support of other concerned persons, agencies, or hospital departments in the goals and the action plan.

4. A Foundation for Evaluation. An initial assessment, revised and updated as needed, allows both the caregiver and the person seeking help to pause from time to time to take stock and see if things seem to be changing in the direction they have intended. By having described the initial situation and the changes they were planning to implement, they have provided the basis for knowing when the plan has been successful and the treatment can stop. Similarly they have provided the basis for discovering that the treatment isn't helping as expected or is making matters worse; for identifying situations where they want to stop and reassess matters and perhaps develop a new plan.

5. A Foundation for Personal Accountability. By providing a foundation for the evaluation of outcome or results, the assessment has also provided a basis for the participants in the contract or covenant to hold one another accountable. In the areas of medicine and counseling, including religious counseling, when the person seeking help is frequently in distress and puts a great deal of trust in another who offers to help, a basis for holding that helper accountable is very important. By providing a foundation for personal accountability, assessment helps those who sought help to consider what role they played in their improvement and to what extent they must credit their caregivers' actions. It provides a basis for their humility and gratitude or, in some cases, their anger and pursuit of justice.

6. A Foundation for Quality Assurance. As I mentioned, one reason for the recent increase of interest in pastoral assessment is the desire of cost-conscious health care institutions for accountability on the part of their chaplains. As Clark Aist looked at the impact of this era on mental health ministry, he saw a need for chaplains to develop a number of assessment-based skills, including "learning to construct audit categories which objectively assess patients' need for pastoral services; . . . evaluating the results of our ministries in light of stated objectives; . . . learning to formulate measurable goals and targeting our time and resources to meet them in cost-effective ways."[25]

Chaplains in all health-related settings, not just mental health, are and will continue to be met with institutional expectations for quality assurance and accountability. It will be difficult to provide that accountability without going back to the work of documenting a spiritual assessment for each patient whom the chaplain cares for.[26]

7. A Foundation for Research. Assessment also provides a foundation for a program of research that enables those in the field of pastoral care and counseling to evaluate its fundamental theories and practices. In order to move beyond basing our pastoral practices on tradition or on global categories, in order to test our various theories about human nature, human vulnerability, and therapeutic processes, as well as the efficacy of spiritual resources, we must begin with assessment. We need the spiritual analogue of the DSM-IIIR's diagnostic categories. With that base we can evaluate whether pastoral interventions, and the theories that guide them, have succeeded or failed.

For Aist the most pressing need in pastoral care is "the need for an integrated corpus of conceptual theory related to pastoral assessment and diagnosis."[27] Only as we develop our knowledge and skill related to assessment will we be able to answer such fundamental questions as, "What are the concrete religious and spiritual problems and concerns that are the special purview of . . . clergy . . . ? What are the symptoms or indicators of these problems? With what frequency do they occur? What spectrum of human behaviors do these problems effect? . . . What kinds of pastoral interventions are most likely to help?"[28]

Improved understanding of and skill in spiritual assessment will allow us to conduct research that begins to answer these questions and others, that enables us to continue to test and revise our knowledge in this field.

8. Assessment as the Touchstone of a Profession's Identity. Spiritual assessment is not just one act among others that pastoral caregivers perform. It is, as Paul Pruyser puts it, the touchstone of a profession's identity, the major tool we use as we practice our profession.[29]

Think of how naturally we associate occupations with specific tools. Carpenters use hammers and saws. Musicians use their instruments. In the traditional helping professions, the identity of the profession and the professional person are at least as profoundly shaped by their diagnostic models and tools as they are by their therapeutic instruments and methods.[30] Our diagnostic tools influence our vision of the factors that contribute to well-being and health as well as to distress and illness. We don't look for, consider, or try to change factors that our diagnostic models don't point to as relevant.

As we move into a period of renewed interest and activity in spiritual assessment, we must move with care. For good or for ill, our diagnostic tools are powerful tools, expanding and constricting our view of what aspects of life pastoral ministry can and should legitimately attend to, expanding and constricting our view of what constitutes good living and what constitutes bad living. I will return to this discussion in chapter 6 when I consider in greater detail the place of power and authority in spiritual assessment.

A Theology of Spiritual Assessment

Before concluding this overview about assessment I would like to provide a brief theology of spiritual assessment. I will do so by referring to three themes: stewardship, justice, and revelation.

Reflection on the sacred dimension of life, on our own life and others', reminds us of some obligations we have. We must be wise in our care for ourselves and others and especially discerning in the face of any problems.

When something seems to be wrong, we must take care to discover what it is and to find a remedy for it. When there are opportunities for enhancing or enriching others' lives, we must respect who they are and work in partnership with them. We must also take care to employ any resources required, including time, in a responsible way. Careful attention to assessment enables us to be good stewards.

Awareness of the power and influence we have in our relationships with one another, especially in explicitly therapeutic relationships, reminds us of our responsibility in our interactions. Specifically we must take care that the power we exercise in relationships with others is guided by a concern for what is good and just. We must be well informed in the aid we offer, in the interventions we propose. We must not use our relationships to gratify our needs at the expense of those who come to us. Finally, we must remain accountable for the consequences of our efforts. All of these goals are facilitated by careful attention to the assessment process.

The emphasis on the importance of assessment is rooted in the conviction that revelation about the divine nature and foundation of existence is continuing and that it proceeds through persons; as the Quakers are fond of saying, "There is that of God in everyone." In this light, assessment is akin to prayer. Attentive listening to another is attentive listening to God.[31] In assessment we are concerned to know how God is at work, in ourselves or in another, and to consider what implications that knowledge has for our lives.

NOTES

1. Throughout the book, all identities have been changed to protect confidentiality.
2. Julia Q. Emblen, Department of Nursing, Trinity Christian College, Palos Heights, Illinois, unpublished study.
3. The model was based on the seven aspects of faith that Pruyser describes in chapter 5 of *The Minister as Diagnostician.*
4. For a larger discussion of how pastors, chaplains, and nurses define spiritual needs, see Julia Q. Emblen, George Fitchett, Carol J. Farran, and J. Russell Burck, "Identifying Parameters of Spiritual Need," *The Care Giver Journal* 8, 2 (1992): 44–50.
5. Clark S. Aist, "The New Shape of Mental Health Ministry," *Cura Animarum* 36, 1 (May 1984): 27.
6. Russell L. Dicks, *Principles and Practices of Pastoral Care* (Englewood Cliffs, N.J.: Prentice-Hall, 1963), 103.
7. Richard K. Young, *The Pastor's Hospital Ministry* (Nashville, Tenn.: Broadman Press, 1954), 119.
8. Pruyser, *The Minister as Diagnostician,* 39. See p. 27 for an even stronger statement of the same concern.
9. Ibid., 39–40.

10. John T. McNeill, *A History of the Cure of Souls* (New York: Harper & Row, 1951), 324.

11. Don S. Browning, *Religious Ethics and Pastoral Care* (Philadelphia: Fortress Press, 1983), 101. See also Browning, *The Moral Context of Pastoral Care* (Philadelphia: Westminster Press, 1976).

12. Charles V. Gerkin provides a more thorough discussion of this shift in *The Living Human Document* (Nashville, Tenn.: Abingdon Press, 1984), 11ff.

13. Sam Keen, *To a Dancing God* (New York: Harper & Row, 1970), 99.

14. This definition is similar to Fowler's definition of faith, "A response to action that precedes and transcends us. . . . The universal human burden of finding or making meaning" (Fowler, *Stages of Faith*, 33). The work of sociologists Glock and Stark has also informed my definition here. See Charles Y. Glock and Rodney Stark, *Religion and Society in Tension* (Chicago: Rand McNally, 1965), 4.

15. See, for example, Fowler's discussion of the differences between faith, belief, and religion, *Stages of Faith*, 9ff.

16. Pruyser, *The Minister as Diagnostician*, 30.

17. Lynda Juall Carpenito, *Nursing Diagnosis: Application to Clinical Practice* (Philadelphia: J. B. Lippincott, 1983), 452ff.

18. Ibid., 451.

19. American Psychiatric Association, *Diagnostic and Statistic Manual of Mental Disorders*, 3d ed., rev. (Washington, D.C.: APA, 1987), xxiii.

20. Ibid., 222.

21. Ibid., 20.

22. Ibid., 190.

23. Heinz Kohut, *The Analysis of the Self* (New York: International Universities Press, 1971).

24. Pruyser, *The Minister as Diagnostician*, 80–81.

25. Aist, "The New Shape," 24.

26. Two helpful resources on quality assurance and pastoral care are *Quality Assurance and Improvement: A Guide to Developing Continuous Quality Improvement Plans in Pastoral Care* (Schaumberg, Ill.: The College of Chaplains, 1992), and The Catholic Health Association of the United States, *Quality Assurance and Pastoral Care: A Development and Implementation Guide* (St. Louis: CHA, 1990).

27. Aist, "The New Shape," 27.

28. Ibid.

29. Pruyser, *The Minister as Diagnostician*, 21ff. In the past ten years our colleagues in nursing have developed a sophisticated model for nursing diagnosis. In that literature the definition of a nursing diagnosis illustrates the close link between a profession's identity and its diagnostic model. "Nursing diagnosis made by professional nurses describes actual or potential health problems that nurses, by virtue of their education and experience, are capable and licensed to treat" (Marjory Gordon, "Nursing Diagnosis and the Diagnostic Process," *American Journal of Nursing*, 1976, p. 1299. Quoted in Mi Ja Kim, Gertrude K. McFarland, and Audrey M. McLane, eds., *Pocket Guide to Nursing Diagnosis* [St. Louis: C. V. Mosby, 1984], 4).

30. In this context see the interesting discussion of how the development of new diagnostic technology has changed the relationship between physician and patient in Stanley Joel Reiser, *Medicine and the Reign of Technology* (Cambridge, U.K.: Cambridge University Press, 1978).

31. This position is similar to Gerkin's and, as he indicates, to Anton Boisen's. See Gerkin, *The Living Human Document*, 37. For a related discussion of the work of verbatims as a modern expression of spiritual meditation, see Russell Burck, "Pastoral Expressionism: Verbatims in the Pastoral Paradigm," *Journal of Supervision and Training in Ministry* 3 (1980): 39–56. Some perspectives on story theology are also similar. For example, see Keen, *To a Dancing God*.

Chapter 2

MRS. GABATINO'S ANGEL

People find that the easiest and most engaging way to begin learning about spiritual assessment is to explore specific cases. In this chapter we will look at the case of a woman, Minnie Gabatino, and her husband, Victor. I will call the hospital chaplain who ministered to Mrs. Gabatino Helen. For the most part the case will be reported in Chaplain Helen's own words.

The Case

Background and Referral

Minnie Gabatino is a sixty-nine-year-old Caucasian woman. She is married. Her primary nurse asked the chaplain to see her. The nurse said she found Mrs. Gabatino "very agitated and anxious" as she awaited tests. She felt Mrs. Gabatino could benefit from a pastoral visit.

Mrs. Gabatino had been admitted to the hospital the previous evening through the emergency room. She had abdominal swelling and pain. In the past she had a hysterectomy for cancer and had been hospitalized at other times for other tests, but the nurse wasn't sure right then what they had been for. The nurse said Mrs. Gabatino's doctor suspected pancreatic cancer, although she was still awaiting tests. A CAT scan was scheduled for that evening.

FIRST VISIT

When the chaplain went into Mrs. Gabatino's room, her husband was there with her. As the three of them chatted, Mr. and Mrs. Gabatino began to share some important parts of their life story. They had been married for forty-nine years. They looked forward to their fiftieth wedding anniversary as a major celebration.

Minnie had a rosary on her bedside table. When asked, she said they were Roman Catholic. They belonged to the same parish for forty-one years and had continued to go there, even after they moved some distance from the parish years ago. Their religious beliefs and practices were very important to them. They said, "We would never miss going to mass." They also said, "People should support their church. What's wrong with people today is they have no sense of commitment." They spoke very highly of their pastor and their friendship with the fine people in their parish.

Minnie said she had an especially strong devotion to the Blessed Mother. She and her husband had a statue of Mary in their garden. They referred to it as a chapel. Mrs. Gabatino shared that on three different occasions when she was sitting alone, quietly, in the garden, she heard Mary speak to her. Minnie said that her daily prayers include reciting the rosary. She would never let anything disrupt this routine. Being in the hospital had not interfered with this practice, but she did have to miss going to mass.

Mr. and Mrs. Gabatino talked about their life together, the things they liked to do. All the things that filled their day, including the housework, gardening, and cooking, they did together. Neither Mrs. nor Mr. Gabatino expressed any interests independent of the other. Minnie knew Victor was disappointed when she was sick and not able to accompany him in their usual daily activities of going to church and to the store. She said that while she was in the hospital he visited her twice a day and called her frequently to let her know where he was and when he was going out and not going to be home.

The Gabatinos had lived in their neighborhood for many years. They spoke highly of their neighbors, some of whom they had known for years. They said they would do anything for their neighbors, and they felt confident they could ask them for anything.

Victor seemed to like to keep the conversation light, interjecting frequent quips and humorous comments. Chaplain Helen began to wonder if his humor was part of his way of diffusing or denying feelings, either his own or his wife's, or both.

As the conversation continued, Minnie described her medical history and her present condition. She expressed concern that another physician she had been seeing had misdiagnosed her condition. She had been referred to a new physician connected to this hospital for another opinion. She expressed concern about the seriousness of her condition. Then the following conversation took place.

MINNIE: So I told Victor, if I die, he should sue that doctor. [The one whom she felt had failed to make the correct diagnosis.]

VICTOR: That's silly. You're going to be fine. They won't know anything until they do the tests.

CHAPLAIN: You're very concerned that this might be very serious.

MINNIE: He's right. We have to wait for the tests. But I think the news will be bad this time.

CHAPLAIN: This time feels different from all those other hospitalizations.

MINNIE: Yes, we really want to celebrate our fiftieth anniversary. I'm afraid I won't make it.

VICTOR: We'll be there! You worry too much. Besides, you have to be there—I can't get another date that night.

The conversation turned light. Minnie told the chaplain what a wonderful sense of humor her husband had, "He always picks up my spirits." They exchanged genuine statements about how much care and concern they have for each other. Minnie talked about what a wonderful guy her husband was. She especially appreciated his understanding about a medical condition she had that had prevented her from having sexual relations with him for many years. "Oh, that's not important," he said. "There's so much more to marriage than that."

As the conversation continued the subject of their dog came up.

VICTOR: Oh, we've always had dogs. We got one when the baby died. It helped her.

CHAPLAIN: You surprised me when you mentioned that you lost a child.

MINNIE: Yes, our daughter.

CHAPLAIN: How old was she when she died?

VICTOR: She died at birth. That was a long time ago. But we're still trying! Right, honey? I keep telling her we should adopt. Maybe about a twenty-five-year-old girl.

MINNIE: He always teases me like that, but he knows I'm the best he can get.

The conversation continued a bit longer. The couple expressed a strong interest in receiving Holy Communion. The chaplain administered the sacrament to them, then concluded the visit with prayer, offering Mrs. Gabatino's concerns about her upcoming tests and diagnosis to the Lord, and asking God's healing presence for both of them.

What do you think was going on in this case? When we ask ourselves that question, we have begun the process of assessment. What would your assessment be of Mr. and Mrs. Gabatino? Based on this initial pastoral visit, what do we know about them? About their general psychosocial background? About their religious or spiritual life? What things are you curious about? What more would you like to know before you made an initial assessment?

For many of us, answering questions like these—thinking in terms of assessments—feels a bit foreign. We're more likely to have a feeling about a case and what should happen next. That approach is not inconsistent with making an assessment. I think for some of us, our assessments are implied in our ideas about what to do next. If you were the chaplain or pastor in this case, what do you think would need to happen next?

The chaplain in this case didn't stop after this first visit to put together a formal assessment. But she thought it necessary to follow up on some of what she had heard in the first visit. She wanted to be able to talk to Mrs. Gabatino when her husband was not present. She wondered if Minnie would then have more to say about her apprehensions. Let's see what happened.

SECOND VISIT

The chaplain returned to Mrs. Gabatino's room later that afternoon, after her husband had gone home. After some initial small talk, the chaplain brought the conversation back to a subject Minnie had mentioned in their first visit.

CHAPLAIN: Mrs. Gabatino, you made a couple of references to dying when I was here earlier [pause]. That's a real concern you have.

MINNIE: [Tears immediately fill her eyes.] I'm so scared. It's not death. I'm not afraid to die. It's Victor. I don't want to leave him. He would not last even one year without me. He'd be so lost. I'm all he has. [She is very much in control, but tears gently roll down her cheeks.]
CHAPLAIN: Your devotion to each other is quite obvious.
MINNIE: He'd be lost. We share everything.
CHAPLAIN: And this illness feels very life-threatening to you.
MINNIE: I just have a feeling. You know, woman's intuition. You know how that is.
CHAPLAIN: [Smiling] Sometimes we do have strong feelings.
MINNIE: [Returning the smile] He's right, of course. We have to wait for the test results.
CHAPLAIN: Sure. It's just hard to deny what you feel inside.

Minnie went on to speak of her love and concern for Victor and how much he meant to her, how they only had each other. She told the chaplain about the death of her husband's only brother in an industrial accident when he was twenty-three years old. She paused as she remembered that, and Chaplain Helen asked about another topic she remembered from their first visit.
CHAPLAIN: And you mentioned that you lost a baby. She was your only child?
MINNIE: Yes, I could never get pregnant again. She died from that SIDS death. You know, crib death.
CHAPLAIN: Oh, I didn't realize. I thought your husband said she died at birth.
MINNIE: Victor always says that. He doesn't like to talk about it. The baby was two-and-a-half months old.
CHAPLAIN: I'm so sorry, Mrs. Gabatino. Tell me what her name was.
MINNIE: Maria, after my husband's mother. It was his favorite name. [There is a long pause.] She was so beautiful, and we loved her so much. We played with her all the time. That night we tucked her into bed together like we always did. [She pauses again and the tears again fill her eyes and roll down her cheeks.] She woke up every morning at five-thirty. We told her that night, "Now, Mommy and Daddy don't get up until seven. You sleep until seven." And we showed her on the teddy bear clock, which is still hanging in her room, "This is seven o'clock." The next morning when we awoke it was quarter to seven. I told my husband, "She's so smart. You watch. She'll call us at exactly seven." It was 7:15; then 7:30. My husband finally went in her room. All I heard him say was, "Oh, my God!" [Her tears continue to fall.] My baby was gone. They tell me she's an angel. [She looks out the window.] But where?

Mrs. Gabatino went on to describe the events following Maria's death. She said she was "too hysterical" to attend the funeral.
MINNIE: The priest took the little coffin on his lap in the car as they drove to the cemetery. He had the baby buried.
Mr. Gabatino put away all the baby furniture and clothes, so she wouldn't have to deal with them.
MINNIE: We go to the cemetery once a year and put flowers on our parents' and his brother's graves and a little toy on her grave. But we don't stay long. I can't stand to be there very long.

CHAPLAIN: I'm sure it's still very painful to think about. Thank you for sharing her story with me.

MINNIE: We never talk about it. I think it's good to talk about it sometimes.

CHAPLAIN: Not talking about things doesn't mean that you don't think about them.

Then Minnie asked to be excused because the medication she was taking to prepare her for her tests was causing her some discomfort. Promising to come back and wishing her well with her tests, the chaplain left.

We could stop the case here and draw our thoughts together in an assessment, but let's move on and see what else the chaplain learned.

THIRD VISIT

The chaplain returned to visit Mrs. Gabatino the next day. She did not yet have the results of her tests, but the possibility of her death was on her mind. She had mixed feelings as she thought about her death. In part, she looked forward to the possibility of being with her baby again. But she was also concerned about leaving Victor—about how he would get along without her.

The chaplain asked Minnie who would take care of her husband if she died: neighbors or friends from the parish, the priest whom she had spoken of in the first visit? Mrs. Gabatino wasn't very sure they would. They didn't reach out to others very much. "We're not the kind of people who do a lot of coffee-klatching," she said. "But," she went on, "it's OK. We have each other."

At first she couldn't think of anyone who would take care of her husband if something happened to her. "All Victor and I have is each other," she said. Then she thought of her foster children. After her baby's death she had been unable to conceive again. So she and Mr. Gabatino became foster parents. They took care of twelve foster children over the years. She loved the children deeply and knew that she had done a wonderful job of raising them. They were all grown now and in successful professional positions all over the world. The Gabatinos had stayed in touch with most of them. She said they praised the care that she and Victor provided for them and were very grateful to them. She is sure that they would do what they could to help Victor if he were alone.

In sharing her feelings about her death, Minnie also said that she felt cheated and let down. She had done what she should in her life and was upset at how things appeared to be turning out for her.

Assessment

Let's leave the case report here and use the information we have to work on our assessment. We'll come back to the case again before the end of the chapter to see how things turned out.

When we make a spiritual assessment, we try to gather together all that we know about a person in order to offer the best pastoral care we can. Our feelings about a person can both inform and distort our pastoral care as well as our assessment. Therefore, I suggest that the first step be to identify our feelings about the person we're assessing.

How do you feel about the people in this case? About Minnie, Victor, the chaplain? I have shared this story about the Gabatinos with groups of colleagues and students. When we talk about our feelings, sadness is frequently mentioned. Many people feel sad when they hear Minnie's words describing that terrible morning when their baby didn't wake up. That part of the story often makes me tearful, even though I've read it many times. I also feel sad when I think of the teddy bear clock, still on the wall, reminding the couple of their loss.

In a case such as this it would be especially important for pastoral workers who had suffered a miscarriage or other infant death to be aware of any feelings from their personal experience that were evoked by being with the Gabatinos.

When people express their feelings about Victor, many are angry with him. They don't like the way his jokes seem to keep his wife from sharing her anxiety about this illness or her grief about Maria's death. I can understand that response to Victor. However, my feelings toward him focus more on how lonely and lost he seems to be with his wife in the hospital.

Although we haven't identified all the feelings that this case might bring out in us, I think we have mentioned some of the major ones. We have also illustrated the point that the assessment process begins with identifying our subjective responses to a case.

Now it is time to describe our spiritual assessment of Minnie. In a case such as this, it would also make a lot of sense to develop an assessment of Victor, or of both the Gabatinos as a couple. Since this is our first spiritual assessment, it will be easier to understand if we limit our attention to Mrs. Gabatino.

To construct a spiritual assessment for Minnie I will follow a model that my colleagues and I developed. The model has two main sections: the holistic assessment and the spiritual assessment. Each of these has seven subsections. This feature has led us to sometimes refer to it as the "7 x 7" assessment model. In the next chapter I will describe the model in more detail. Right now we'll simply follow the sections and subsections to summarize our assessment of Mrs. Gabatino.

We actually begin the assessment by reviewing any information that was part of the **referral**. In this case we remember that the nurse indicated Minnie was having some tests done to determine whether or not she had cancer of the pancreas, a life-threatening condition. The nurse had also described Mrs. Gabatino as "agitated and anxious."

Holistic Assessment

The holistic assessment section begins with a summary of key **medical information**. In Minnie's case, the medical facts are significant. There is a possibility that she has a life-threatening form of cancer. Her history of treatment for cancer might make this an even more serious risk. That treatment included a hysterectomy. She also makes a reference to infertility after her first child and to medical causes that prevent her from having sexual relations with her husband.

The next information we note focuses on Minnie's **psychological state**. The nurse described her as agitated and anxious. In the chaplain's visits with her, anxiety and grief seem to stand out. However, these moods are understandable or appropriate given her medical situation and her history. Mrs. Gabatino also shows other moods, including warmth and concern for her husband, and some peaceful acceptance of her possible death.

An assessment of **family systems** is the next section in this model. We don't know anything about Mrs. Gabatino's family of origin, but we do know a good deal about her marriage and something about her relations with her foster children. The Gabatinos have been married for forty-nine years. Minnie looks forward to their fiftieth wedding anniversary as a major milestone. There is a remarkable closeness between Minnie and Victor. They appear to do everything together and seem uncomfortable when separated. In the marital relationship, Minnie does not have much opportunity to express feelings such as anxiety or grief. Her husband steps in quickly to lighten the mood, and she doesn't object. The Gabatinos have twelve now-grown former foster children. They apparently stay in communication, but Minnie doesn't seem to feel close to them or comfortable with placing any demands on them.

Our assessment continues with consideration of the **psychosocial** aspects of the case. We don't have exact information but it appears that the Gabatinos are retired, middle-class people. They don't seem to have any anxiety about coverage of the costs of this hospitalization. They own their own home in an older suburb and have lived there for quite a few years. Despite her long-term relatedness to a neighborhood and a parish Minnie does not appear to have close friends or family. Attending church and tending to household maintenance with her husband appear to be some of the most important activities in her life. We have no information about any other interests, hobbies, schooling, or whether Minnie was ever employed.

From a developmental perspective, Minnie is in a period of life known as older adulthood. Psychologist Erik Erikson has described the tasks of this stage of life as addressing integrity over against despair.[1] This description seems to fit Minnie. As she faces the possibility of being diagnosed with a life-threatening illness, she is reviewing important moments in her life. She appears, for the most part, to be affirming the value—the integrity—of her life.

As we continue with our holistic assessment, we review what we know about Mrs. Gabatino's **ethnic and cultural** background. From her husband's name and from what we know about their parish, we might guess that both

Minnie's and Victor's parents or grandparents were from Italy. She has some characteristics we associate with that ethnic heritage, including the importance of her Roman Catholic faith and the importance of her family.

The last section in our holistic assessment looks at the **societal issues** in the case: to what extent Mrs. Gabatino's suffering is caused by or compounded by dysfunctional social institutions or cultural patterns. From Minnie's perspective there do not appear to be any major public issues. Colleagues who have reviewed the case from a feminist perspective suggest that Minnie's life has been heavily influenced by the norms and practices of our patriarchal culture. They point to her unresolved grief over her only biological child and to her submission of her emotional needs to her husband as illustrations of this.

At this point our holistic assessment has been completed and we are ready to consider the seven sections of the spiritual assessment in similar detail.

Spiritual Assessment

The first area we will consider in our spiritual assessment has to do with **beliefs and meaning**. Mrs. Gabatino describes herself as a devout Roman Catholic. She undoubtedly finds that much of the meaning in her life is derived from her faith. From her conversation with the chaplain, we can see that she holds at least some, and probably many, traditional Roman Catholic beliefs. She believes in a life after death, for example, and says that knowing that she will see her infant daughter when she gets to heaven is part of why she is not afraid to die.

She has a special devotion to the Blessed Mother, who like Mrs. Gabatino, knows the pain and grief of losing a child. Minnie also appears to believe that one of the attributes of God is that God is just and rewards those who are obedient. In light of this, she expresses frustration that she has led an upright life, yet her reward has been grief at her child's death, her inability to have another child of her own, and now possibly terminal cancer.

The next aspect we consider in our spiritual assessment has to do with **vocation and consequences**. Minnie's meaning in life may also depend to a considerable extent on fulfilling what she believes are her sacred duties—her vocation. The roles of mother and wife appear to have been central in her life. Undoubtedly, Roman Catholic teachings about a woman's fulfillment being expressed in these roles has been important in Minnie's dedication to them.

As we hear Mrs. Gabatino's story, we also hear how both of these roles have been threatened. Minnie does not think of her twelve foster children as her children, nor as part of her family. It is as if in her eyes, with the death of her baby, she was never able to fulfill her duty to be a mother. Now she faces the possibility of a terminal illness, and her attention is focused on how she will not be able to fulfill her obligations as a wife.

In this section of the assessment we should also note the importance of morality for Mrs. Gabatino. It is important to her to lead an upright life, and she expresses some dismay that so few people seem to share this value nowadays.

Next we consider that aspect of spiritual assessment that we call **experience and emotion**. We are actually interested in two different aspects of spirituality here. The first is whether Mrs. Gabatino has ever had any direct religious experiences. In the first visit, we learn that she has; that the Blessed Mother has spoken to her three times. Second, we are interested in the overall feeling that accompanies Mrs. Gabatino's description of her faith. Despite her immediate anxiety and her painful grief, she communicates a predominantly peaceful, confident mood in what she shares about her faith.

Another aspect of spiritual assessment is **courage and growth**. Our interest here is directed toward any indications Minnie gives of times of change in her faith and of the possibility that the present crisis might be such a time for her. Minnie's faith story, at least as far as we have been able to learn about it, seems remarkable for its stability. We've heard almost nothing about times of doubt, struggle, or conversion. Rather she has told us of how constant and steady a resource her faith has been for her in the past, as well as in the present.

Rituals and practices are the next area we consider. Mrs. Gabatino appears to have a rich ritual life. She practices daily private devotions, which include reciting the rosary. She and her husband attend mass on a regular basis. Receiving Holy Communion from the chaplain is important and comforting to her. In addition to these daily and weekly rituals, we have learned that Mr. and Mrs. Gabatino make an annual visit to their daughter's grave at the cemetery. Their wedding anniversary is an important annual event for her, and their fiftieth anniversary is certainly something she is looking forward to. In contrast to her present participation in this rich ritual life, it appears that she did not participate in the rituals surrounding her baby's death. While that may be unfortunate, it was probably typical of the practice in such situations when she died forty-seven years ago.

One of the important aspects of our spiritual assessment focuses on Mrs. Gabatino's **communities** of shared belief, meaning, and ritual. One senses some complexity here. She has long-standing relations with her parish and neighborhood, which would suggest rich interpersonal ties in these contexts. But as she continues to describe these relations they seem distant and formal. She and her husband don't socialize—"coffee-klatch"—much with their neighbors. In a similar fashion, she has raised twelve foster children but doesn't seem to have close contact with any of them. Her connection with her parish is also threatened by a diocesan plan to have it merge with a nearby parish. When she speaks of Victor and says, "All we have is each other," it seems she has accurately described her rather circumscribed community of shared belief, meaning, and ritual practice.

The final area for spiritual assessment is **authority and guidance**. In times of doubt or of crisis, where does Mrs. Gabatino turn for support and direction? Minnie's faith appears to be a rich resource of guidance for her. Its teachings are the framework she uses to understand what is happening to her and what her duties are. Her prayers may be a way she expresses her needs for guidance. It is harder to know what persons, if any, help her interpret how her prayers are being answered. We don't know if she talks with her priest very much, or with Victor, or whether she listens within herself to hear how her prayers are being answered.

To a large degree, Minnie is able to listen within herself to hear the answers to her prayers. We get the impression from other things she says that she has some sense of her own inner authority. Her husband's cheerfulness notwithstanding, she has an intuition that her test results will bring bad news. Her inner authority seems to have been at work in her decision to leave the physician whom she felt had misdiagnosed her case.

Looking more directly at her religious life, I deduce that she has internalized the traditional teachings of her church. Its authority doesn't operate as something outside her but as part of her own values. However, during one moment in the second interview I hear her express doubt about those teachings. It comes at the end of her story about Maria's death. Looking out the window she says, "They tell me she's an angel. But where?" This poignant question reveals an inner experience in tension with the authority of her faith—a faith she has affirmed as her own.

At this point we have said a lot about our assessment of Mrs. Gabatino. Is there more that should be noted? Yes, I think there is. You may see things that I haven't included in this summary. When I have talked about the case with students and colleagues, many other possibilities have been mentioned. For example, there may be some links between Mrs. Gabatino's infertility, other gynecological problems, and her unresolved grief over Maria's death.

In our assessment we might also make note of what we don't know—of the areas where we have some questions and would like to learn a little more. For example, I am curious about Mrs. Gabatino's grief over the death of her baby. I would like to know if she thinks a lot about that loss or whether it is on her mind right now because she is facing the possibility of her death. There are other things that I would like to know to help me as I plan my pastoral care with Minnie. However, our situation in ministry frequently calls on us to begin to respond whether we have all the information we would like to have or not. With Minnie, I need to be ready to work with the information I have and see if the opportunity arises to learn more or ask further questions.

The extensiveness of what we have said in the spiritual assessment of Mrs. Gabatino makes a **summary** of our assessment an essential step before we develop our care plan. How would you summarize what we have said about her? This is what I would say.

> Minnie Gabatino is a sixty-nine-year-old Caucasian woman. She was admitted to the hospital for tests following abdominal pain. She has a history of being treated for cancer, including a hysterectomy. The present tests are intended to see if any further cancer has developed.
>
> Minnie has been married for forty-nine years and is very close to her husband, Victor. She lost one natural child in infancy. With her husband, she was a foster parent for twelve other children. She does not appear to have many close contacts with any of these children, with other family, or friends.
>
> Minnie is a Roman Catholic, and her faith is a very important part of her life. She prays daily, and attends mass regularly with her husband.
>
> Minnie is apprehensive about the results of her tests. She says she is not afraid to die, but she is concerned about who would care for her husband. Her present situation has revived memories of the death of her infant daughter forty-seven years ago.

Up to this point our discussion has focused on the chaplain's assessment of Mrs. Gabatino. But it is very important not to let that assessment keep us from listening to her **self-assessment**. Before I develop my care plan, I need to review what Minnie would say about herself and, most important, what she would say about her spiritual needs and resources at this point.

In the visits with the chaplain, Mrs. Gabatino was very direct in sharing her self-assessment and in describing her current spiritual needs. She said she was apprehensive about the test results. She said she was not afraid to die, but that she was concerned about who would take care of Victor. She said that her faith was an important, sustaining resource for her. She also welcomed the chaplain's visits and asked her to come back.

When I put all this together, what kind of **pastoral care plan** does it add up to? Let's answer that question from two perspectives: from the perspectives of the hospital chaplain and her parish priest.

My care plan for Mrs. Gabatino would be quite similar to the one that appears to have guided her chaplain: listening to her, developing a trusting and supportive relationship with her, and inviting her to share her story and her feelings. As the relationship begins, I don't know whether or not she will be faced with bad news from her tests. If I can develop a supportive and trusting relationship while we're waiting for the test results, then I can be more helpful and supportive if she has to deal with a crisis.

I would make sharing prayer and Holy Communion a regular part of our time together. These spiritual practices are familiar and helpful to Minnie. I would encourage her to use them and would develop a relationship with her that includes sharing them together.

I would ask Mrs. Gabatino about her parish. I'd like to support that connection if it is important now, and possibly strengthen it if I could. Does her priest know she's in the hospital? Would it be all right with her if I called him to let him know she was here? Is there a eucharistic ministry program or other lay visitation program that would arrange to visit her while she was in the hospital or convalescing at home?

Finally I would try to arrange a time when Mr. Gabatino and I could talk privately, perhaps over a cup of coffee. I'd like to get to know him better. I'm interested in seeing to what extent his lighthearted behavior is meant to keep her spirits up and to what extent it is his way of coping with stressful times such as these. I'd like to begin to develop a relationship that would be a support for him, especially if his wife's test results show that she does have cancer. I'm also interested in learning more about any other support he has for himself and in doing what I can to encourage him to use those supports or develop some if none exist besides his wife.

Many of my students and colleagues have felt that the pastoral care plan should also focus on helping Minnie express her fears and doubts, such as she did when she said she wasn't sure about where her angel-daughter was. Others have felt it important to address the pattern in the couple where Victor's humor appears to keep Minnie from expressing her feelings. I think these are legitimate areas of concern. I would continue to observe them and gather information about them. But as a hospital chaplain, unless I was sure that we would have an opportunity for a longer relationship, since Minnie didn't focus on them as needs, I would not take any initiatives with them.

If I were the Gabatinos' parish priest, however, these are the two places where my care plan might be different from the chaplain's. Hopefully a trusting relationship already exists between Minnie and the priest, and she will be able to express her fears to him and to receive an empathic response, as well as the support of the sacraments. Building a network of support for both Mrs. and Mr. Gabatino with other members of the parish is important. It is also important for the priest to spend time alone with Victor to develop a relationship with him at this stressful time.

As their priest, my decision to invite Mrs. Gabatino to talk more about her doubts or to talk with the couple about how Victor's humor cuts off her feelings would be based on my assessment of how important those goals were for them, how much stress they are coping with from her diagnosis, and what I know about the recurrence of their patterns in these areas.

Now that we've developed our spiritual assessment and care plan, let's return to the chaplain's case report and see what actually happened.

FOURTH VISIT

The next day the chaplain, on the way to a meeting, met Victor in the hall. With a smile, he said they had gotten the test results back and everything was negative. His wife was about to be discharged. He was here to take her home. The chaplain expressed her delight at the good news they had received, explained that she had to attend a meeting, and expressed her regret that she would not be able to say good-bye to Mrs. Gabatino personally before she left. The chaplain asked Victor to give Minnie her best wishes.

The case ends a bit abruptly. The patient is about to be discharged, and the chaplain is not free to see her before she goes. Unfortunately this situation is not uncommon in hospital ministry, especially with all the pressures that exist to keep hospital stays as short as possible. Each time I read this part of the case I wish the chaplain had been able to see Minnie personally to celebrate her good news and to say good-bye. They had shared together at a significant level, and it feels as though their relationship needed to have some closure. Maybe the chaplain was able to give Minnie a phone call that day or the next to share with her in the good news and to say good-bye.

Even though the case ends abruptly, it ends on a positive note. The test results are negative. The life-threatening cancer Minnie was afraid they would find wasn't there. Perhaps you join me in hoping that in the years that followed, Minnie has remained healthy and the couple had a wonderful celebration of their golden wedding anniversary.

The next chapter will take a closer look at the spiritual assessment model which we used to reflect on this case.

NOTE

1. Erik Erikson, *Childhood and Society*, 2d ed. (New York: W. W. Norton, 1963). See esp. 247–74.

Chapter 3

THE 7 × 7 MODEL FOR SPIRITUAL ASSESSMENT

I sometimes call the model used for Minnie Gabatino's spiritual assessment a functional, multidimensional model. But that title is too long. Because the model focuses on seven holistic dimensions of assessment and seven spiritual dimensions, I also call it the 7 × 7 model, or 7 × 7 for short.

Work on the 7 × 7 originated in the fall of 1985. Julia Quiring Emblen, a professor of nursing at our hospital, wanted to give surgical nurses a tool they could use to assess their patients' spiritual needs. She talked with the hospital chaplains, first with Russell Burck, later with me, knowing that we might have some helpful resources.

Julia, Carol Farran (another member of the nursing faculty), Russell Burck, and I discussed the strengths and weaknesses of the various approaches to spiritual assessment with which we were familiar. None of them was quite what we would recommend. The four of us met regularly for more than two and a half years. During that period we developed a set of guidelines for evaluating models of spiritual assessment. Those guidelines and their use in evaluating some models of spiritual assessment are the topics of chapters 6 and 7.

Our work led us to develop our own approach to spiritual assessment, the 7 × 7 model. Under Julia's leadership we also carried out a research project on the ways different professionals, primarily nurse educators, identify spiritual needs. Our regular meetings and collaboration came to an end in 1988. The results of our work during that period have been presented at a number of professional meetings and have been reported in a number of publications.[1] Ironically, although we accomplished a great deal, we never developed the simple spiritual assessment tool that Julia originally requested.

Beginning Assumptions

Early in our work on the 7 × 7 model, we made important decisions about six aspects of our approach to spiritual assessment, which I review here.

The setting in which we were working, a large, urban, university-related hospital, played a part in two decisions about our model. The first was the decision to employ a **functional approach** to spiritual assessment. This approach focuses more on **how** a person makes meaning in his or her life than on **what** that specific meaning is. Here are two questions that illustrate the functional approach to spiritual assessment. "What is the most powerful or important thing in your life?" and "What things do you believe in or have faith in?"[2] James Fowler's work on stages of faith development is probably the most familiar example of this approach to spiritual assessment.[3] Our appreciation for Fowler's work was a factor in our choosing this approach.

The alternative to a functional approach in spiritual assessment is known as a substantive approach, which focuses on whether a person holds certain specific beliefs. An example of this approach can be found in the assessment model of physician Elisabeth McSherry. In that model one of the areas assessed is the person's image of God. McSherry's assessment uses a three-point scale to rate people in this area: E = Early, God is like their own parents; M = Mature, God is seen and experienced with some biblical understanding; and U = Unformed or undeveloped, there is no idea of God.[4]

McSherry's model makes use of specific Christian beliefs about God. Its focus on beliefs is what makes it a substantive approach to spiritual assessment. We felt that a substantive model, regardless of religious orientation, would employ assumptions that would not be shared by the diverse patients and staff of our institution or most similar hospitals. For that and other reasons, we chose to base our 7×7 model on a functional approach.

Our hospital setting made our next decision quite natural. We decided that spiritual assessment should be explicitly placed in the context of a **whole person assessment**. This approach is standard in pastoral care and nursing. Our research group knew the significant role that culture, family, personality, and health plays in spiritual well-being. Therefore we chose to develop a spiritual assessment model that took into account the whole person, both as an individual and as a part of larger family, social, and cultural systems. The multiaxial approach to diagnosing mental illness of the American Psychiatric Association's Diagnostic and Statistical Manual, Third Edition, Revised, provided a basis for our explorations into multidisciplinary aspects of assessment.[5]

Our third decision was to take a **multidimensional approach** to the religious or spiritual dimension of assessment. Some models of spiritual assessment are one dimensional, asking only, for example, about religious affiliation, that is, what church or synagogue a person belongs to. Other one-dimensional models focus only on a person's religious or spiritual practices, how often the person prays or attends religious services, for example.

We felt, by contrast, that it was important to know something about a number of key dimensions of a person's religious or spiritual life. Our model focuses on the dimensions of religious beliefs, experiences, practices, interpersonal relations, and change. Three distinct areas of religious belief are included in our model.

As we worked on the model, we changed the number of spiritual dimensions we included and their content. We were guided in our decisions by our professional experience. What things had we found it most important to know in order to provide pastoral care? We were also guided by the classic description of the multidimensional nature of religion by sociologists Charles Glock and Rodney Stark and other literature in the field.[6]

The fourth choice we made was about the **method of gathering information**. Did we want to use a list of questions, or did we prefer a less structured process? Our preference was to have a model that wouldn't require changing key elements in pastoral care as we understood it.

The approach to pastoral care that we favored focused strongly on developing a trusting relationship with the person to whom care is offered. In the context of that relationship, pastoral ministry enables people to share their stories, express their needs, if any, and work with the caregiver to find the spiritual resources for addressing those needs. In this tradition, allowing people to share their stories or express their needs in their own words is very important.

Our approach to spiritual assessment is consistent with this approach to pastoral care. In this method, the pastoral conversation proceeds as it normally would. After the meeting or visit has concluded, our model provides guidelines for organizing the information obtained in the visit, thus equipping the chaplain or pastor to provide effective pastoral and spiritual care.

The fifth assumption that shaped our work was that we were not developing a new instrument for spiritual assessment. Rather our aim was to develop a **framework** to organize the information that might come from a pastoral interview or through use of another spiritual assessment tool. The purpose of our framework was to draw attention to the areas we thought were important to consider in a comprehensive spiritual assessment. Within each of those areas we felt there were a number of existing models that might provide the specific content for assessment of that dimension, or new models could be developed.

An example will help clarify this. The first dimension we review in our spiritual assessment is the person's beliefs and the ways that person finds meaning in life. A pastoral worker who wanted a structured way to organize information about a parishioner's or a patient's beliefs and sources of meaning could employ one of many different options. H. Newton Malony's Religious Status Interview, based on Pruyser's work, would be one such option.[7] It considers a person's beliefs regarding providence, grace, and faith, among others. Another option is Elisabeth McSherry's model, which attends to a person's beliefs about his or her relationship to God, image of God, and the presence or absence of faith and hope.[8]

The sixth decision we made as we started our work was to develop a **conceptually sound approach** to spiritual assessment. As we reviewed other spiritual assessment models, we found many whose underlying theoretical structure was inadequate. Our aim was to develop a model with a solid conceptual base, comprehensive in its definition of the spiritual dimension of life and applicable in as many different ministry settings as possible. We felt it was important to accomplish this task first. At a later time we hoped to devote attention to making our model more useful for clinical practice or research.

Content of the 7 × 7 Model

As you saw in our assessment of Minnie Gabatino, the 7 × 7 model has two major subdivisions and seven dimensions within each. The rest of this chapter will describe each of the dimensions in the model, how we define that dimension, and why we chose to include it in the model. Some of the dimensions in the model will be more familiar and easier to understand than others. Figure 1 provides a summary of the model which shows how it is organized.

Holistic Dimensions

Our spiritual lives in general and our spiritual needs and resources at any particular moment are strongly influenced by what is happening in the rest of our life. The power of these dimensions to influence our spiritual well-being is one reason for attending to them in the process of spiritual assessment.

But there is another reason as well. Our spirits are not separate from our bodies, our emotions, and our thoughts. Each of us is one whole person. Our ways of thinking about ourselves often limit us to considering only one dimension at a time, but that does not mean those dimensions are separate

FIGURE 1. The 7 × 7 Model for Spiritual Assessment

Holistic Dimensions	The Spiritual Dimension
Medical Dimension	Beliefs and Meaning
Psychological Dimension	Vocation and Consequences
Psychosocial Dimension	Experience and Emotion
Family Systems Dimension	Courage and Growth
Ethnic and Cultural Dimension	Ritual and Practice
Societal Issues Dimension	Community
Spiritual Dimension	Authority and Guidance

or discrete. Our wholeness, the way in which the spiritual aspects of who we are are expressed in all aspects of our lives, requires that spiritual assessment be whole person assessment. When I begin spiritual assessment, therefore, I first review the information I have about all aspects of the person's life.

The first holistic dimension I consider is the physical or **medical** dimension. My concern here is whether what is happening in the person's life at this level is having an impact on his or her spiritual well-being or functioning. This is usually readily apparent. Major changes in health, such as a stroke and subsequent paralysis or a below-the-knee leg amputation related to diabetes, frequently have noticeable effects on a person's spiritual life.

Sometimes concerns at the biological level emerge from not what has happened but what might happen. Mrs. Gabatino's possible diagnosis of pancreatic cancer is an example of this. Determining whether or not episodes of memory loss are early signs of Alzheimer's disease is another example. Physical or medical assessment is also important in caring for persons who have disabilities.

A person whose mood or behavior has changed without obvious cause should also be encouraged to have a thorough medical assessment. Such changes can be caused by different things, including disease, diet, and reactions to medication. Pastoral care will take different directions depending on whether someone is dealing with a temporary and easily reversible biological change or with a severe, permanent, or even progressive loss of physical health.

In this dimension of holistic assessment the pastoral worker's role is usually adjunctive. In most cases he or she may do little more than make a referral for medical attention if that has not already taken place. Sometimes the role may include helping people make choices about treatment options for themselves or a loved one. Sometimes the role may include advocacy with the health care system or its workers on behalf of people who are not being treated justly.

Next I consider three closely related dimensions of psychosocial functioning; the psychological, family systems, and psychosocial. Our model reviews each of the three separately, but they can be grouped together.

In considering the **psychological** dimension of people's lives, I would like to know if they are currently being treated for any psychological problems and what that treatment consists of. I want to know something about their personality and their general approach to life. I am also interested in knowing if they have had any major psychiatric illness, and if so what it was, how it was treated, and how it was resolved.

My experience tells me that any problems people are having in this area of their lives will often have a major impact on their spiritual lives and needs. It is important for pastoral workers to be aware of such problems if they exist, to work in tandem with any mental health professionals these people are seeing, and to make referrals for careful psychological assessments if problems in mental health are suspected.

The next dimension of holistic assessment is from a **family systems perspective**. This area is familiar to many pastoral workers, and some may have received advanced training in it. This perspective helps us focus on the way an individual's present problems may be shaped by the relationships in that person's family, either their current immediate family or patterns traceable back over several generations.

The **psychosocial perspective** is the next aspect of holistic assessment in our model. Our colleagues in social work employ this perspective on a routine basis. Here I am interested in knowing about the person's past and present. Where was this person born and raised, who was in his or her family, what were childhood, adolescence, and adulthood like for this person, were there any major crises in those years? In the context of this perspective I am interested in how much schooling a person completed and in his or her employment history.

This perspective also focuses where people are in the present. What is their current living situation, where do they live, is their housing adequate, with whom do they live, what are those relationships like, and are they responsible for other people? I am interested in what they do with their time, if they are working what kind of work they do and whether they find it fulfilling. I am interested in other things they do with their time and whether they have any important leisure interests. I am also interested in their financial resources and whether these are adequate to meet their needs.

The next aspect of holistic assessment considers the person from the perspective of **race, ethnicity, and culture**. Our racial and ethnic backgrounds have a strong influence on our behavior. The assessment process needs to include this perspective in order to appreciate people in this context and to avoid inappropriately imposing values from one's own culture.

The sixth dimension of holistic assessment in the 7 × 7 model is called the **societal issues perspective**. This perspective is the least familiar to most caregivers and often the most difficult to explain. It is a way of checking to see if any of the person's distress is being caused by or compounded by dysfunctioning and oppressive social and cultural systems.

The most powerful diagnostic tools of traditional helping professions explain the causes of people's problems in terms of the individual person, his or her body or his or her behavior. Although these approaches are helpful, they don't take into account the possibility that the "sickness" of a social institution or a cultural pattern is causing or contributing to a person's misery. If we neglect this societal issues perspective, we run the risk of looking for individual causes for social and cultural problems, of blaming the victims. We include the societal issues perspective in our holistic assessment as a way to get the fullest possible picture of the person and his or her situation and to avoid creating a diagnostic perspective that forces us into individual-level explanations for social and cultural problems.[9]

People who are at a power disadvantage in our society, including women, racial minorities, those with low incomes, and those with disabilities, are at a greater risk of suffering from social or cultural oppression. In working with these people, the caregiver will do well to include a careful societal issues assessment.

The Spiritual Dimension

We have completed a review of the first six holistic dimensions in the 7 × 7 model. Now I would like to describe the categories the model uses to assess the seventh dimension, the explicitly spiritual dimension of human life.

The first aspect of spiritual assessment in the 7 × 7 model focuses on **beliefs and meaning**. This explores the ways the person finds meaning and purpose in his or her life. Some people are able to express directly the sources of meaning and purpose in their lives. Some use religious language to describe that meaning, others don't. Some people would say, for instance, that knowing they are children of God gives life meaning. Others would attribute their sense of purpose to their enjoyment of life.

Sometimes people cannot say in a few short sentences what gives their lives meaning and purpose, but they can tell a story or two about themselves. In those stories they convey what gives their lives meaning. Paying attention to objects that have symbolic significance for someone can be a helpful way to learn about the important beliefs and ways that person finds meaning in life. For some those objects may be related to religious traditions, a religious picture or statue, for example. For others the objects that symbolize the important meaning in life may be nonreligious, a family heirloom or summer home, for example.

How a person handles the symbolic nature of religious objects and language is another point that I consider in this aspect of the spiritual assessment. The framework of Baldridge and Gleason, based on Tillich, is simple and useful.[10] They describe three approaches to the use of religious symbols: literal, broken myth, and restored myth. This framework has a lot in common with Westerhoff's four-stage framework and Fowler's description of the stages of faith development.[11] The work of Ivy on styles of spiritual consciousness and Weiss's adaptation of it are also worth mentioning here.[12]

Attending to what people say about what gives their lives meaning, however, is not always the best way to find out how they handle religious meaning. People also convey important information about what gives their lives meaning by their behavior, by what they do with energy and vitality, and by what they avoid doing. If a caregiver wants to know what gives people's lives meaning and purpose, he or she can listen to what they say about that but can also watch how they live their lives and then make inferences from that. Sometimes a caregiver will find that what people say about the meaning in their lives is consistent with how they behave, and sometimes it will be obvious that it is not. A caregiver may observe sources of meaning that the people themselves are not aware of. They might even disagree if someone pointed out what they had seen. This is what it means to take a dynamic perspective on the spiritual dimension of life. We take seriously both what people tell us and what we observe, which may or may not be consistent with what they have told us.

In learning about another person's beliefs and meaning, it is also important to attend to any significant changes that have occurred in those beliefs. Further, it is important to know about any current situations that threaten to disrupt important sources of meaning. As we saw with Minnie Gabatino, much of the meaning in her life came from caring for others, for Victor and for her foster children. If she became ill and was unable to care for Victor, and in fact had to depend on him to help take care of some of her daily needs, it could be a severe threat to the way in which she finds meaning and purpose in life and could thus cause significant spiritual distress.

For many people, the ways they find meaning in life are shaped by past and present contact with religious traditions. In this dimension of the spiritual assessment I want to know if the person has participated in any religious traditions in the past or is participating in any at present. I want to know how that participation has shaped that person's beliefs and the way he or she finds meaning in life.

The next aspect of spiritual assessment in the 7 × 7 model focuses on a person's **vocation and consequences**. These are the duties and obligations that a person feels called to fulfill. This aspect is closely linked to the previous one, beliefs and meaning. Sometimes our sense of the duties and obligations in life, what we should do, stems consciously and directly from the beliefs that give meaning to our lives—that is, our sense of duty is a consequence of the beliefs we adhere to. At other times the connection may be more unconscious or indirect. As we saw in Mrs. Gabatino's case, her Roman Catholic faith, as well as her Italian background, played a role in instilling in her a sense that her role or vocation in life was to be a wife and mother.

In this aspect of the spiritual assessment I also reflect on people's sense of right living, the shoulds and oughts that shape their behavior and the judgments they make about their and others' behavior. Minnie believed people should be loyal supporters of their churches. "What's wrong with people today is they have no sense of commitment," she said. Many religious traditions have specific prescriptions and prohibitions on behavior. My assessment here focuses on the role these play in the life of the person I am assessing.

My interest includes a sense of whether people feel they are fairly able to fulfill the duties and obligations that are important to them, or whether they are frustrated or guilty about being unable to fulfill them. In pastoral situations where a person is going through a change or crisis, it is important to be sensitive to changes in his or her perception of being able to fulfill these duties and obligations. In other situations, where a person's motivation seems blocked, where he or she seems unable to fulfill important goals, it is possible that the person feels a duty to suffer or make a sacrifice. Potential growth in meeting expectations could be seen as conflicting with the need to find meaning through suffering and sacrifice; therefore an impasse could result.

The third aspect of spiritual assessment in the 7 × 7 model explores **experience and emotion**. This portion of the assessment attends to the person's reports of any direct encounters with the divine or the demonic. Survey research indicates that about 30 percent of people in the United States claim to have had a core spiritual experience.[13] In this category we would include near-death experiences. People who have had such experiences are often hesitant to reveal them to others. However, we know from those who have described them that these experiences often have a profound and lasting effect on their lives. In this regard, Mrs. Gabatino's story of hearing Mary speak to her when she was meditating by her statue in the garden seems characteristic. Direct contacts with demonic or evil powers seem to be less common, but they are no doubt at least as equally powerful in their impact on a person's life.

The 7 × 7 model also focuses on the overall emotional tone of the person's spiritual life. This may be strongly influenced by the direct religious experiences a person has had, if any. It is a summary of the emotional tone that accompanies the person's living out of his or her sense of the meaning of life and the consequent duties and obligations. This mood has consistency over time, despite the emotions that may come and go in response to passing events. It is easy to confuse this aspect of the spiritual dimension with the holistic dimension of psychological assessment described earlier, but they are distinct.

Let's look at Mrs. Gabatino again in order to understand this better. In the previous chapter I said that I thought she displayed overall a peaceful and confident spiritual mood despite the simultaneous presence of what I would describe as a psychological mood of anxiety. I base this description on the centeredness I sensed when she talked about her death and not being afraid to die. But the picture may well be more complex. I also got a sense of a more constricted mood in Minnie as she complained about people's lack of commitment nowadays.

I am still looking for a framework that will increase the precision and consistency of this aspect of the spiritual assessment.[14] In the meantime I have found certain words to be useful in summarizing the predominant affect in a person's spirituality. Those words include grateful, serene, joyful, stoic, timid, worthless, angry, guilty, and exhausted.

The next aspect to be considered in the 7 × 7 focuses on the person's **courage and growth**. My use of the term *courage* in this context has been influenced by Paul Tillich's use of it in his classic book *The Courage to Be*.[15] What I have in mind is not a matter of being brave or tough in threatening situations. Rather it is the ability to enter into spiritual doubt, to tolerate times when we reject as false or inadequate some or all of what we have previously believed, not knowing if a new sense of belief will emerge to take its place. It is the courage to enter the dark night of the soul. It is also the courage to experience a conversion, a turnaround, a breakthrough.

Another way to look at this is to observe what a person does when new life experiences challenge existing beliefs. Must people disavow the new experiences in order not to have their beliefs threatened? Must people strain their perception of new realities, or existing beliefs, in order for them to fit? Or can they let go of the existing beliefs, even when it is unclear what new beliefs might emerge to provide security?

Can the person entertain the possibility of new beliefs? Does his or her history reveal a capacity for spiritual growth or development? If so, has that growth been slow and gradual, or more sudden? Have there been experiences of spiritual rebirth or conversion? Or has there been an arrest in the growth of faith, or a long, sustained plateau?

In developing the 7 x 7 model we did not incorporate faith development as a norm. We prefer instead a more descriptive approach, seeing whether there is evidence of change and growth in a person's spiritual life, and if so, attempting to describe it.

The next aspect of spiritual assessment in the 7 × 7 model focuses on **rituals and practices**. Here my attention is directed to any rituals or practices that give expression to a person's sense of meaning and purpose in life or that are part of their fulfillment of their sense of their duties and obligations. These rituals and practices may be related to traditional religion, for example, the importance of attending mass regularly for Mr. and Mrs. Gabatino. They may also include activities that are not traditionally religious but that none-theless are significant expressions of what makes life meaningful. In the next chapter we will see how the annual gathering of the extended family for a holiday dinner is an example of such an activity.

In the assessment of rituals and practices it is important to note any important changes. It is also important to determine if any significant changes are about to happen that would interfere with a person's ability to perform the rituals and practices. While she was in the hospital, Minnie appeared to be coping with not being able to attend mass with her husband. Being able to receive communion at the bedside probably helped her compensate for this loss. If she had had to face a lengthy hospitalization, this change in her ritual life might have been more distressing.

The next aspect of spiritual assessment focuses on a person's **life in community**. This portion of the assessment asks whether the person is part of one or more formal or informal communities of shared belief and meaning in life, shared ritual and practice. Mrs. Gabatino appeared to have two main communities. One of the communities of shared belief, meaning, and ritual for Minnie was her Roman Catholic parish. She and her husband had remained connected to it for years, despite a move to another neighborhood. The other community for Minnie was her relationship with her husband. In some cases where a person participates in more than one community of belief and meaning, tension may exist between the beliefs, practices, and duties associated with the two communities. In Minnie's case, there appeared to be harmony and considerable overlapping of beliefs and values between her two communities. In this portion of the assessment it is important to determine to what extent the communities a person is a part of might be resources for support in times of need. Are they large and vital communities, or are they threatened and depleted? Are they flexible, resourceful, and adaptive, or defensive and rigid? In Minnie's case, both of her main communities were under some threat. In her marriage, aging and illness could precipitate serious loss in what appears to be her most significant community. Her parish was in an old inner-city neighborhood and was slated for merger and closing by the diocese as part of its effort to responsibly manage its resources.

Other interests in the area of a person's community are worth considering too. What role, for instance, do people typically play in their communities of shared meaning and purpose? Are they open, guarded, or conflicted? Can they give and receive affection and support in any of their communities? Based on his reading of family systems theory, Laurel Burton names four roles a person may typically take in a family or a familylike group. They are mover, opposer, follower, and bystander.[16] This can be a useful structure for this portion of the assessment. In Mrs. Gabatino's case, I have the impression that she was able to give care and support in her primary, marital, and family community, but that she was not able to ask for or receive much support in either her family or faith communities, or in the neighborhood where she lived.

The final aspect of spiritual assessment in the 7 × 7 model focuses on **authority and guidance**. Three apects are important to me in this portion of the assessment. First, I am interested in knowing if the person will give me enough authority to enable me to help him or her, if needed. Second, I am interested in knowing if the person looks upon himself or herself as having some authority to help meet the questions and challenges of life. Third, I would like to know what other significant sources of authority there are in this person's life that must be considered.

The question of authority is linked to several of the aspects of the spiritual life that have already been described. It focuses on where people find the authority for their beliefs, for their meaning in life, for their sense of vocation and duties, and for their rituals and practices. The question of authority comes into central focus when people face times of conflict between duties or beliefs, or when they face doubts or confusion. Where a person turns for comfort and guidance at such times tells us a good deal about where spiritual authority resides for him or her.

One common place people look to for authority and guidance is a special text, including traditional religious or holy books. They may also seek it in persons. Some may be ordained or otherwise consecrated persons, some may be trusted mentors, family, or friends. Some may be worthy, and others unworthy, of the authority and trust that have been given to them. People may also see themselves as having the inner resources and authority with which to meet the challenges they face. People who look to several different authorities may find them diverging at a particular point. It is important to consider this in assessing this dimension of a person's spiritual life.

There are a number of frameworks in the literature which can be employed to give further structure and specificity to this aspect of spiritual assessment. Kenneth Pargament has a simple but useful model of three styles of authority: deferring, self-directing, and collaborative.[17] Fowler's work on stages of faith includes a dimension that assesses relations with authority.[18] In our early work developing the 7 × 7 model we found Dorothee Soelle's discussion of the stages of muteness, lament, and solidarity to be useful in reflecting on the extent to which a person felt able to have authority, a voice, in times of conflict and doubt.[19]

When we look at Minnie Gabatino, two important authorities can be noted in her life: the teachings of her church and her own voice. As we noted in the previous chapter, considerable harmony appears to exist between these two authorities. Minnie has internalized the teachings of her church; its beliefs, values, and practices have become her beliefs, values, and practices to a significant degree.

In the next two chapters I will apply the 7 × 7 model to two more cases.

NOTES

1. George Fitchett and J. Russell Burck, "A Multi-Dimensional, Functional Model for Spiritual Assessment," *The Care Giver Journal* 7, 1 (1990): 43–62; Carol J. Farran, George Fitchett, Julia Q. Emblen, and J. Russell Burck, "Development of a Model for Spiritual Assessment and Intervention," *Journal of Religion and Health* 28, 3 (Fall 1989): 185–94; George Fitchett and J. Russell Burck, "A Model of Spiritual Assessment," *The Care Giver Journal* 5 (September 1988): 144–54, and Julia Q. Emblen et al., "Identifying Parameters."

2. Clifford C. Kuhn, "A Spiritual Inventory of the Medically Ill Patient," *Psychiatric Medicine* 6, 2 (1988): 87–100.

3. Fowler, *Stages of Faith.*

4. Elisabeth McSherry, "Semi-Structured Interview," 3, and "Computer Data Information Sheet," 1. Elisabeth McSherry, Brockton/West Roxbury VA Medical Center, West Roxbury, Mass.

5. APA, DSM-IIIR.

6. Glock and Stark, *Religion and Society in Tension.*

7. H. Newton Malony, "The Clinical Assessment of Optimal Religious Functioning," *Review of Religious Research* 30, 1 (September 1988): 3–17.

8. McSherry, "Semi-Structured Interview."

9. Further elaboration of this perspective can be found, among other places, in Howard Clinebell, *Basic Types of Pastoral Care and Counseling*, rev. ed. (Nashville, Tenn.: Abingdon Press, 1984), esp. 25–45; and in Ivan D. Illich, *Medical Nemesis* (New York: Pantheon Books, 1976).

10. William E. Baldridge and John J. Gleason, "A Theological Framework for Pastoral Care," *Journal of Pastoral Care* 32, 4 (1978): 232–38. Gleason has updated that model in "Spiritual Assessment and Pastoral Response: A Schema Revised and Updated," *Journal of Pastoral Care* 44, 1 (Spring 1990): 66–73.

11. John H. Westerhoff III, *Will Our Children Have Faith?* (New York: Seabury Press, 1976), esp. 79–103; Fowler, *Stages of Faith.*

12. Steven S. Ivy, "A Faith Development/Self Development Model for Pastoral Assessment," *Journal of Pastoral Care* 41, 4 (December 1987): 329–40; Fredric S. Weiss, "Pastoral Care Planning: A Process-Oriented Approach for Mental Health Ministry," *Journal of Pastoral Care* 45, 3 (Fall 1991): 268–78.

13. Jared D. Kass, Richard Friedman, Jane Leserman, Patricia C. Zuttermeister, and Herbert Benson, "Health Outcomes and a New Index of Spiritual Experience," *Journal for the Scientific Study of Religion* 30, 2 (June 1991): 203–11.

14. The work of Roy Nash may be a helpful resource here. See Nash, "Life's Major Spiritual Issues," *The Care Giver Journal* 7, 1 (1990): 3–42.

15. Paul Tillich, *The Courage to Be* (New Haven, Conn.: Yale University Press, 1952). Although he does not use the term *courage*, Fowler describes a similar process (*Stages of Faith*, 31).

16. Laurel A. Burton, *Pastoral Paradigms* (Washington, D.C.: The Alban Institute, 1988), 24ff.

17. Kenneth I. Pargament et al., "Religion and the Problem-solving Process: Three Styles of Coping," *Journal for the Scientific Study of Religion* 27, 1 (March 1988): 90–104.

18. Fowler, *Stages of Faith*, 241ff.

19. Dorothee Soelle, *Suffering* (Philadelphia: Fortress Press, 1975).

Chapter 4

ETHEL'S LAMENT

I have known Ethel for more than five years. During the first two, Ethel was hospitalized three times for psychiatric treatment. My assessment of Ethel's needs changed and developed during those two years. However, for purposes of this report, my spiritual assessment will focus on where Ethel was at the end of that period.

Because I work as a chaplain in an acute-care hospital, my pastoral relationships with patients tend to be relatively brief. The average length of stay for our patients is slightly more than one week. But many of our patients, like Ethel, have chronic conditions with multiple complications, and we see them during many hospitalizations over many years. Thus, although the context of the chaplain's ministry is different from the parish pastor's, it is hoped that the spiritual assessment here will be as relevant for parish pastors as it is for hospital chaplains.

The Case

Background and Referral

When I first met Ethel, she was sixty-seven years old. She was a patient in the adult general psychiatric unit at the hospital. She was being treated for depression and suicidal ideation. She had asked for a chaplain to visit, to pray with her, and to offer some support.

Ethel is a Caucasian woman of English descent. Her husband, Ed, had died the previous winter, just eight months before her hospitalization. He had been disabled and confined to bed for many years prior to his death. Most of the time he lived at home. Periodically he was hospitalized for special tests or treatment. Ethel had cared for him at home, where he died. At the time of his death, Ethel and Ed had been married thirty-nine years.

Ethel and Ed have a daughter, Anne, and a son, Charles. Charles has been in the navy for fifteen years and lives overseas. Ethel is proud of his accomplishments but rarely communicates with him. Anne lives in a nearby suburb. She is divorced and remarried. At the time of Ethel's first hospitalization, her relationship with Anne was quite strained. It improved later.

Anne has one daughter, Veronica, by her first marriage. Ethel and Veronica have a better relationship than do Ethel and Anne. Veronica was, at that time, a high school student. On her way home from school, she would periodically stop at Ethel's house and visit with her grandmother to see how she was doing.

Ethel lives in a working-class suburb in the home that she owns. She and Ed lived there for many years, and she has been active in many community and civic groups.

Ethel has been a member of a local, mainline, Protestant church for many years. In the years prior to Ed's death they didn't get out to church much. They were a "shut-in" couple. The pastor and members of the church would visit them at their home. The pastor reports that he felt very close to both Ethel and Ed.

Ethel suffers from several physical health problems. She has had diabetes for fifteen years and takes insulin. She takes medication to help regulate her blood pressure and has had some kidney problems. She also has some chronic arthritis and back pain, for which she takes medication.

First Hospitalization. Ethel came to the hospital because her diabetes was out of control, and attempts to adjust her medication were not successful. In the course of her medical hospitalization Ethel was found to be severely depressed, with suicidal ideation. She was transferred to the psychiatric unit. A central issue that came into focus in the following days was whether Ethel's medical condition was so unstable that she would need to be moved to a nursing home. There was concern that she would not be able to live at home independently. Ethel was very upset when she was informed of that possibility. The thought of moving to a nursing home and losing the family home caused her great distress. She was also depressed and grieving Ed's death. She was not sure that she had anything to live for.

During this hospitalization Ethel dealt with some of her grief at Ed's death. She demonstrated some resolve to go on living. Her depression improved somewhat with medication and therapy. Her suicidal ideation diminished and was no longer a problem. Further changes in her medication led to the stabilization of her diabetes. Ethel was discharged from the hospital after four weeks with outpatient follow-up to her psychiatrist for her medications.

Her pastor, the Reverend Mr. Smith, was very supportive. He often came to the hospital to visit with Ethel, to help keep her connected with the church and to pray with her. He was also active in assisting with plans for Ethel's care following discharge. Throughout Ethel's hospitalization he said that if it was hard for Ethel to live at home alone, people from the church would arrange to do what was necessary to help her.

During this hospitalization, I was only moderately involved in care for Ethel. I tried to facilitate some expression of her grief over Ed's death. I tried to help Ethel find meaning in life without Ed. I helped integrate Pastor Smith into the treatment team and helped the team see him as an important resource in this case. I prayed with Ethel. To my surprise, after her discharge, Ethel kept in contact with me. She periodically called me to say that she was doing fine and that she was keeping up with her appointments with her psychiatrist. She said she was finding some meaning in living and was doing all right.

Second Hospitalization.   Fifteen months later Ethel had a second crisis. Ethel's granddaughter, Veronica, had become pregnant. Even though Veronica and her boyfriend, Tony, quickly got married, Veronica's mother, Anne, didn't want to have anything to do with them. Since Ethel's house had a basement apartment, Veronica and her new husband moved there. The whole extended family was in a state of crisis. Ethel called and asked me to assist in finding a clinic that would provide prenatal care for Veronica. My efforts to locate a resource that the family could afford were not successful, but Ethel finally found one, using her own network of friends and contacts in the community.

A month later, just a few days after Christmas, Ethel called. There had been an argument in the family. Ethel was beginning to set some house rules regarding care of the apartment and utility bills. Tony had complained about these rules. Anne had said to Ethel, "It will be your fault if Tony leaves Veronica."

Ethel had made plans for a wonderful, warm family Christmas dinner at her home. Instead there had been a big argument and the dinner did not happen. When I talked with her, she had already called her friends and the pastor. But she said she felt that everyone would be better off if she were gone. Several days later she took an overdose of her pain medication. The pastor brought her to the emergency room, and she was hospitalized again.

The focus of this hospitalization was a little different from the first. It now seemed important to begin to sort out the family dynamics that appeared to be linked to this episode. Ethel was initially resistant to family therapy. She thought that talking about things in the family would only make them worse. The staff didn't think things could get much worse and encouraged Ethel to give it a try.

A social worker met with Veronica and Tony and later also with Anne and Ethel. Tony was not acting very responsibly. Ethel was concerned about this but was not sure she should be the one to speak to him. Veronica was not happy with his behavior either but was unable to confront him. The social worker's session with Veronica and Tony appeared to be somewhat productive. The social worker confronted him about his responsibilities as a husband, tenant, and soon-to-be father, and he apparently listened. His behavior was much improved for quite a while thereafter. However, Veronica's difficulties in expressing her needs in that relationship were not addressed.

The goal of the session with Ethel and Anne was to help them improve their communication about what they expected of each other and how they handled conflicting views about that. Ethel reported that the session was not very helpful. They ended up upset with each other, and no further sessions were scheduled.

During this hospitalization, the staff also tried to get Ethel to focus more on her own life. They tried to help Ethel see that Veronica was having a lot of problems Ethel couldn't help with. Veronica would have to deal with them herself. Ethel needed to find some activities and interests for her life separate from Veronica's life. The staff talked with Ethel about what she might get involved with, and Ethel began to think about that and make some plans.

Ethel was discharged after four weeks. A referral was made for follow-up family therapy. Ethel was also encouraged to continue her medications and her visits with the psychiatrist.

During this hospitalization, Pastor Smith was as active and supportive as he had been during the first hospitalization. He went to Ethel's home when she called him and said she wanted to die. He brought her to the hospital, visited her there several times, brought her news of the congregation, read Scripture, offered prayer, and helped make an important referral upon discharge.

During Ethel's second hospitalization I took a bit more active role than I had in the first. I suggested to the team that we address family systems issues along with Ethel's depression. In our time together, Ethel talked with me about her distress over the situation in her family, about her desire to make things better, but her feeling that whatever she did just made things worse. My response was to be empathic and supportive. I talked with Ethel about the importance of the family sessions and the importance of having her own activities. We talked about what she might find rewarding in life now that she no longer had Ed to care for, and we talked about the need for her to decrease her involvement in Veronica's affairs.

In the subsequent months, things went fairly well for Ethel. She was exploring her own activities. Family relationships were improving. They made some efforts to engage in outpatient family therapy, but basically that referral did not work out.

Third Hospitalization. A few months later, three days after Easter, Ethel called me and said she was leaving town and planning not to return. She also had a kidney infection, and she was not going to take any of the medication that had been prescribed to treat it. She did not want to hurt anymore, she did not know what to do, and she wanted to die. There had been another argument between Ethel and Anne over the baby shower and who was going to buy what for Veronica's baby. Plans for a family Easter dinner had not materialized because of a big family argument the day before Easter. Four days after Easter, Ethel was back in the hospital.

In this hospitalization there was more focus with Ethel on her suicidal ideation. She was also less cooperative with the unit's rules than before and tested limits and rules about where she was allowed to go in the unit. She seemed to be making gestures related to escaping from the unit. She was confined in seclusion on two occasions for failure to cooperate with the staff and follow rules related to where she was allowed to be in the units. Overall, this hospitalization was different from her previous ones.

Gradually, with adjustments in her medication and continued milieu treatment, Ethel's behavior improved. The family conflict seemed to diminish. Ethel's sense of self-worth was improving. She was discharged after seven weeks. Her discharge plan included follow-up visits with her psychiatrist to monitor her medications and a referral for outpatient pastoral counseling to explore how she handled issues of conflict and anger in her family, as well as issues about her self-worth.

In the third hospitalization I sensed that issues of grief about Ed's death were contributing to Ethel's depression. I thought it would be helpful if she could express her feelings about this loss, particularly her anger with God for all the terrible things that had befallen her. I suggested to Ethel that it was important for her not to hold all these feelings in, but to express them. Later, it seemed to me that these suggestions had not been too helpful. They seemed to have increased Ethel's anxiety and may have been part of why she was not cooperating well with the rest of the treatment team. I discontinued that approach and supported the management and structuring of feelings that was being encouraged by the rest of the treatment team. This new approach seemed to work out well.

After discharge, Ethel twice saw the pastoral counselor to whom she was referred. One month after her discharge from the third hospitalization, Ethel's great-grandson, Benjamin, was born. After the baby's birth Ethel stopped seeing the pastoral counselor. She has not been involved in any other counseling since then. Ethel has not had any further suicidal ideation or thoughts since the baby was born. Her mood is vastly improved, and her sense of meaning in life is dramatically sustained by caring for baby Ben, who lives with his parents in Ethel's basement apartment.

Yet Ethel's life has not been without problems since Ben's birth. She has been in the hospital several times for various medical conditions and also has had some outpatient surgery. Her medical problems are numerous, but none of that has had a negative effect on her mood.

Eight months after baby Ben was born, Ethel was at the hospital for an appointment. I went to see her in the clinic. She told me that one of the things that gives her deep satisfaction is rocking Ben to sleep. As she rocks him she says to him, "You and I have a little secret, Ben. You saved my life and I saved yours." The first reference seems easy to understand. The child's birth has given Ethel a renewed sense of meaning and purpose in life. The comment also appears to refer to the fact that Ethel intervened early in Veronica's pregnancy when abortion was one of the options being discussed.

Assessment

In developing the spiritual assessment for Ethel I follow the same outline that I used in the assessment of Mrs. Gabatino in chapter 2. The first step is to become aware of our own **feelings** in order to account for how they might influence our assessment. How do I feel toward Ethel and toward the other key people in the case? I like Ethel. I have a lot of respect for her. She is a loyal, loving, and generous person. I am impressed by her care for her family and by the network of friends she maintains contact with and is concerned about. Ethel is aware that some people tend to write her off as simple and complaining. But I eventually learned that she doesn't complain without good reason. In fact she takes some pride in being self-reliant and independent. Ethel has maintained a caring and gentle spirit despite major illness in her life, in Ed's life, and despite crises in her family.

I have not met the other members of Ethel's family. I know them through her, and so my feelings toward them are colored by her feelings toward them. I feel concerned and protective toward Veronica. She seems to be a kind, hard-working girl who is struggling with some significant issues. I do not like Anne or Veronica's husband, Tony. They seem selfish and irresponsible. Ethel's son, Charles, is quite removed from the family, physically and emotionally, so he does not really affect the family dynamics.

The other person in the case whom I have met is Ethel's pastor. I respect him. He has been concerned, available, and resourceful in the face of a prolonged and frustrating series of crises in Ethel's life. He has provided support to Ethel at times of acute suicidal crisis, he has driven her to the emergency room when she needed to be admitted to the hospital, he has provided pastoral support at the hospital and at home. I admire his commitment and his patience.

Before I move into the holistic assessment, let me review the **referral**. In this case, the request for pastoral care came directly from Ethel. Her request was for a chaplain to visit, pray with her, and provide support. She made this request when her diabetes was seriously threatening her ability to return to live in her home. This was a very upsetting time for Ethel. She spoke critically of the medical resident who introduced this possibility and persisted in discussing it with her. I think her request for support from a chaplain was in part a request for an ally who might help her and her pastor fight this resident and convince the staff that she could return to her home safely.

About the time of each subsequent hospitalization, Ethel also initiated contact with me. She called me from her home, sharing her suicidal thoughts and feelings. In each case I urged her to follow her psychiatrist's advice and come into the hospital, and I assured her that I would see her in the hospital as soon as I could.

Holistic Assessment

I have reviewed the background of Ethel's case, my feelings about Ethel and the other people involved here, as well as the specifics of the referral for pastoral care. With that preliminary work accomplished, I am ready to begin the more focused aspects of the spiritual assessment. Our 7 × 7 model begins with the first dimension of the holistic assessment, the **medical aspects** of the case.

As I mentioned in the background of the case, Ethel has a complex medical history. She has diabetes, which requires oral insulin and attention to her diet. She has arthritis and takes medication for this condition. She also has cataracts. A lot of Ethel's time and energy is focused on her health. Treatment of any of these conditions or any new problems is always complicated and prolonged by the presence of the other problems.

Ethel is attentive to her body and its signals. She distinguishes between familiar pain and symptoms from existing problems and new pain or symptoms that may be unfamiliar. Ethel has an excellent relationship with her primary physician. He is available to see her whenever she needs him. He listens to her descriptions of her concerns and takes them seriously in his diagnostic and treatment plans. She has a great deal of confidence in him. Ethel's relationships with the specialists to whom she has been referred have usually not been as good. They often have not listened to her as patiently and carefully or have ignored her comments.

In Ethel's case, the **psychological perspective** is also significant. She has suffered from major depression. She has had suicidal thoughts and made suicidal gestures. These have been treated quite successfully with inpatient psychiatric hospitalization and its supportive milieu, as well as with medication.

Ethel also shows evidence of having a a borderline personality. People with this type of personality have a poorly consolidated sense of self. Under stressful or threatening conditions they experience a fragmentation of that self. When people like Ethel try to restore a sense of control in the face of threats or stress, they often behave in a demanding way. They also rely heavily on the psychological defense known as splitting. In this process, complex or ambiguous situations are reduced to simpler situations. In Ethel's case we see this in her descriptions of her physicians. There is her "good" internist who does what she wants and there are the "bad" specialists who do not behave the way she would like them to. She has a similar attitude toward her family members.[1]

Some of Ethel's treatment plan attempted to address this underlying borderline personality. The hospital's supportive atmosphere was designed to reduce her level of stress and anxiety. The referral for pastoral counseling was designed to continue that support. I hoped that it might bolster her sense of self-esteem and help reduce her tendency toward fragmentation in the face of conflicts with family members. The efforts at family therapy were also made partly to give Ethel an opportunity to learn more effective ways to communicate with her family, especially when she was feeling under stress or threatened.

In Ethel's case the next aspect of the holistic assessment, **family systems issues**, follows from the previous discussion. Losses (Ed's death) and conflicts in her immediate family were closely linked to Ethel's episodes of depression, suicidal ideation, and hospitalization. The birth of her great-grandson brought a significant improvement in Ethel's mood and psychological well-being.

Ethel's relationship with her family seems to be characterized by what family therapists call a lack of differentiation or boundaries. Ethel seems to be overinvolved in the lives of family members. This is most evident in the difficulty Ethel has in letting Veronica struggle to learn to confront and communicate with her husband, Tony. It was also seen in Ethel's expectation that the other members of her family would share her view of the importance of harmonious holiday family dinners.

Family therapists find that family problems often persist from one generation to the next. I know little about Ethel's family of origin, but she did tell me that her father was an alcoholic and that the years after his death were the best years of her mother's life. From a family systems perspective, it also appears that after Ed's death, Veronica responded to her grandmother's suicidal depression by becoming pregnant and bringing new life into Ethel's world. If this perspective is correct, we might predict that the next period of stress for Ethel may come when her great-grandson gets older and begins to assert some independence.

The next aspect of the holistic assessment is the **psychosocial**. Unfortunately I know little about Ethel's childhood or early adult life. She was raised in the Midwest and has one brother. As mentioned above, her father was an alcoholic. As an adolescent and young adult, she was very interested in religion. She attended church regularly and even enrolled in several courses at a Bible training institute. She had some interest in becoming a Bible teacher but apparently received little encouragement in that direction.

Instead Ethel married Ed. They established a home in a suburb, where Ethel still lives. They had two children. During this time, Ethel also spent time caring for her mother in the later years of her life. Ed was disabled in World War II. Ethel worked as the family's breadwinner for a while, making crafts that were sold through a shop run by a local civic organization. She takes some pride in telling this part of her life story, as well as pride in her handiwork. In her middle adult years, Ethel was active in the woman's auxiliary of the local VFW post and was its president for several terms. In the years before his death, Ed was at home as an invalid, and Ethel's primary activity was caring for him.

Next, our assessment focuses on Ethel's **ethnic, racial, and cultural** background. As I have noted earlier, Ethel comes from a white, Anglo-Saxon, Protestant background. The values of middle America—family, hard work, and self-sufficiency, home, neighborhood, and nation—are important to her. She also illustrates some aspects of the traditional women's roles in this culture. We see this in her devotion to care for others and the way she sacrifices her own needs and interests to the service of taking care of others.

The final aspect of the holistic assessment is the **societal issues perspective**. Do any social or cultural-system problems or failures contribute to Ethel's problems? I think at least two societal issues may be significant in Ethel's case. The first is the reduced choices she has regarding her health care as an older person depending on Medicare. Ethel is not able to go to any specialist she wants. She must find one who accepts Medicare reimbursement. This posed a problem when we tried to make referrals for outpatient family therapy and pastoral counseling for Ethel. Moreover, Ethel does not drive and is not able to walk for long distances, so finding services that were convenient was a requirement that further complicated her treatment.

A second societal issue that appeared to be a factor in Ethel's case was the patronizing attitude of some of the specialists she consulted. As I have already mentioned, more often than not the specialists to whom Ethel was referred took the position that they, not she, knew her needs best. Ethel did not like this attitude. When they ignored her contributions, it not infrequently turned out that they were wrong and she was right. I consider this a societal issue, and not just a personal shortcoming on the part of the individual specialists Ethel consulted. I see this as behavior that is unfortunately widespread and upheld by cultural norms about men and women, about professionals and laypeople, and about older people. In this context, one might also make the case that some of Ethel's problems stem from or are exacerbated by the patriarchal nature of our culture and the consequences of that for women's self-esteem and ability to be assertive.

Ethel has some awareness of the impact of the first of these societal issues on her situation. She complains about the limitations imposed on her health care choices by her dependence on Medicare. When she voiced such complaints, she often asked me, somewhat rhetorically, if what she was expecting was unreasonable.

Spiritual Assessment

Our model for holistic assessment now proceeds to spiritual assessment, to an explicit description of Ethel's religious and spiritual life. The first dimension we consider in the formal spiritual assessment is the person's **beliefs and values**. Ethel did not say much about her explicit religious beliefs. She was raised in a mainline Protestant church and she has been a member of a local congregation in the same denomination for all of her adult life. Ethel believes in God and she prays to God. During her most depressed times she feels neglected by God and also feels that she has lost her faith in God. When things are going better in her life, she feels a return of faith and hope.

Although Ethel said little about her explicit religious beliefs, she did say a lot about what gives her life meaning and purpose: her family. The times when she wanted to die were after Ed's death and when there was conflict in her family. Renewal of meaning and purpose in her life have come from family harmony and especially from the birth of her great-grandson. Caring for this child and for Veronica seem to be important sources of meaning in Ethel's life at present.

What do we see when we turn to the dimension of **vocation and consequences** in Ethel's life? Again, Ethel did not explicitly say very much about any sense of duty, obligation, or vocation that she felt may have been derived from her religious beliefs. It is evident, however, that Ethel finds meaning in the role of caretaker. She took primary care of her mother in her last years and days. She took care of her disabled, ill, and dying husband. She raised two children and is currently helping to care for her granddaughter and new infant great-grandson. Further, Ethel's care for others has not been limited to her immediate family. As a member and leader of a local civic organization, she helped provide monthly recreational activities for patients at the local VA and long-term care hospitals.

What about a duty or obligation to care for herself? Ethel seems to have no explicit sense of obligation to care for herself or to pursue fulfillment of her potential. She gets uncomfortable when the idea is suggested to her. Appeals to a theological basis for caring for oneself as well as one's neighbor had no impact on Ethel. At one point when her diabetes was more stable, she had an eye examination and got new glasses. With her vision improved she entertained the idea of getting a driver's license and buying a car. I asked her what she would like to do if she had a car and could go places in it. She was not interested in using the car for her own pleasure, for trips, to see friends, or to go shopping. She thought it would be useful to take Veronica and the new baby to the doctor.

Ethel's discomfort with doing things for herself seems continuous with her difficulty in being direct when asking others for help and expressing her needs. She is generous and fair in her treatment of others, and she implicitly expects to be treated in a similar fashion without having to ask or make her needs known. When this expectation is disappointed (for example, when Anne does not offer to drive her to a doctor's appointment), Ethel becomes very upset.

Ethel seems most comfortable asking for care or help from health professionals, including the hospital chaplain and especially her supportive internist. Since it is the duty of these professionals to be helpers, Ethel is apparently able to make more explicit demands on them, although she does occasionally also seek help from her pastor.

The third dimension of our spiritual assessment reviews Ethel's **religious experiences and overall emotional tone**. On several occasions, Ethel told me the story of the night before one of her surgeries twelve years ago. She was very anxious that day. She went to the hospital's chapel and prayed. She reported that after her prayer she felt God came close to her and gave her assurance that everything would turn out fine. Her anxieties went away. They were replaced by calm assurance. Ethel did not share any other reports of direct experience with God.

Research by Jared Kass has suggested that people who have experienced a "core spiritual experience," such as Ethel's, will have reduced anxiety and an increased sense of purpose in life. Further, Kass believes that when people are upset, it is possible to help them recover the sense of assurance or peace that usually accompanies core spiritual experiences through relaxation and guided imagery.[2] Although this was apparently a powerful and reassuring experience for Ethel at the time it occurred, it has not provided her with a more enduring sense of serenity in the face of subsequent problems. In fact it was during times when she was feeling better that she recalled it. Unfortunately at that time I was unaware of Kass's work and never tried to see if recalling the experience would be a source of assurance during the times when she was upset.

The other theme we review in this dimension of the spiritual assessment is the predominant mood or emotion accompanying the meaning and purpose, duties and obligations of Ethel's life. During the first two years I knew her I observed no overall, consistent emotional tone to her religious or spiritual life. Rather she appeared to alternate between states of despair and delight, depending primarily on the state of cohesion and harmony in her family, and to a lesser extent on the current status of her health.

Next we consider the dimension of **courage and growth** in Ethel's life. In the time I have known her, Ethel has not shared any account of changes in her religious beliefs or practices. She has not had an experience of gradual or sudden conversion, nor has she communicated any sense of development in her religious or spiritual life. What is more obvious is stability and consistency over many years in the way she finds meaning in life and in her beliefs and practices.

Ethel gives the impression of being open to growth and advice, but when that possibility is explored, she becomes resistant. For example, Ethel believes that to love someone means you also must agree with that person. So when Anne or Veronica have an argument with her, it doesn't mean they have a difference of opinion. It means they do not love her. Ethel did not want to talk about the possibility of there being another way to understand love. She was not interested in the possibility that love for family or for God could include disagreement, argument, conflict, apology, forgiveness, or reconciliation.

A similar pattern was evident when her health professionals, including myself, took a position she disagreed with. It meant we did not care for her or did not love her. It was also evident in Ethel's beliefs regarding her sense of vocation. She did not believe that doing something for herself could be an expression of self-love or self-worth that might be pleasing in the eyes of God, and she was rather closed to exploring the issue.

The next dimensions to consider are the **rituals and practices** that express the central beliefs and meanings in Ethel's life. First we can look at formal religious rituals or devotional practices. In recent years Ethel has rarely attended worship at her church, even though most of this time she has been physically well enough to do so and rides would have been readily provided for her. She does not appear to miss the services. When I asked her about this, she was vague in describing why she did not attend. She did not mention any other communal religious practices. I also have the impression that she does not follow any regular pattern of private devotional practices. In the times of crisis surrounding her hospitalizations, she has mentioned praying to God and her difficulties with that.

In Ethel's case it also seems important to inquire into the religious rituals that were available to sustain her at the time of Ed's death and in her subsequent grief. I have no information about his funeral and what that was like for Ethel. I was struck that on the second anniversary of Ed's death, Ethel had no other way to mark the occasion except to call me on the phone and talk with me about the special nature of the day and the sadness she was feeling. She had no special prayers to say, no pilgrimage to church or cemetery, and no community to mark the day with her.

If we broaden our perspective beyond the ritual activities usually associated with religion, some other interesting themes emerge. Consistent with the importance of family in Ethel's life, family rituals are very important to her. Her second and third hospitalizations occurred just days after Christmas and Easter, respectively. On each of those occasions, Ethel had plans for gathering the whole family for a (ritual) meal and holiday celebration. On both occasions, the wished-for family gathering was canceled because of major arguments among family members the preceding day. The rituals were important to Ethel but unfortunately not to her family.

At the same time as Ethel travels less and less often to church, she travels more and more often to doctors' offices, emergency rooms, and the hospital. While Ethel is less often in church to bring her concerns before God, she is more often following the ritual protocols of doctors' appointments and hospital admissions, describing her chief complaint and medical history to a doctor, therapist, or nurse—following the routines of testing and treatment. I wonder if one set of rituals is replacing the other.

The next explicitly spiritual dimension that we consider is the **community** with whom Ethel shares her sense of meaning and purpose in life, and with whom she shares the rituals that celebrate and confirm it. We have already noted that Ethel is formally a member of a local Protestant congregation, to which she has been connected for many years. She is not currently active in that community. She does not appear to have any significant personal ties to other members of the church. She has told me of close friendships with others in the church in the past. I met one such friend, who has since died. Ethel has been close to the church's previous pastors, as she is to the current one, who actively reaches out to care for Ethel.

Ethel's family impresses me as the most significant community in her life, but I have the impression that her family does not hold a similar view of the importance of their relationships with one another or with Ethel. This is also a community that has undergone major changes. Ethel lost a key member of her community, her husband, Ed. She has also gained an important new member, Veronica's new baby, Ben. Thus Ethel's most important community is unstable, unpredictable. Furthermore it is a community with serious conflicts. The relationship between Ethel and Veronica is harmonious, but almost all the other relationships have significant tensions or are remote. Despite Ethel's deepest wishes, her family is not a community of shared belief and meaning.

Is there any significant community for Ethel beyond her church or family? Ethel maintains some ties with the civic organization she was active in, but these seem quite minimal. She does have friends and agencies whom she calls on to provide practical support with travel to medical appointments. When Ed was ill, neighbors helped paint the house and put a new roof on it. During the Christmas season around her second hospitalization, Ethel received five turkeys and two other boxes of food from community agencies. She takes some pride in being a part of a community where neighbors look out for and care for one another as they do for her.

I wonder if something parallel to the changes in her ritual life might be taking place in Ethel's community of shared belief and meaning. Perhaps a community of professional helpers is developing around Ethel's medical problems: a group that legitimates her periodic need for care and attention for herself, a community where she can be dependent without feeling such conflict about it.

In this dimension we also want to make note of Ethel's style of being in community. Independent of the specific community she is part of, is there a pattern to how Ethel relates to others in community? I have already mentioned that the dominant role or vocation in Ethel's life appears to be that of caretaker. This pattern also seems to describe how Ethel relates to others in the important communities in her life. She is a generous, hardworking woman, and in all the communities of her life she has taken leadership and has rolled up her sleeves and gone to work to care for others. It is significant to note that when she does this, it is often without being asked. Yet at the same time, she expects others to reciprocate. Thus Ethel believes that her labors spent caring for others have earned her the right to expect them to reach out and respond to her needs, and, again, without her having to make those needs explicitly known. It is around this unspoken assumption of reciprocity of attention and care that Ethel becomes privately disappointed and bitter and her relationships in community become conflicted.

The final dimension of our spiritual assessment looks at how **authority and guidance** operate in Ethel's life. This aspect of Ethel's life is complex and requires careful attention. Ethel can be quite dependent and deferential. She gives the impression of being uncertain and lost and eager for direction and guidance. This pattern is most evident when she is in acute crisis. For example, during the first week or so of her last hospitalization when she was very depressed, she was unable to pray and asked the chaplain to pray for her. At times she said she did pray and that her prayer to God was "Thy will be done." It was a passive prayer and not a prayer of surrender, such as the prayer of Job that followed his demand to know why God had afflicted him or the prayer of Jesus that followed his plea "Let this cup pass from me."

Ethel has a considerable measure of inner authority. She knows what she wants. She knows what she thinks is right and what should be done. But she has difficulty expressing her authority, especially in situations of conflict or tension. In such situations she will behave in a passive manner, and if the conflict is severe enough, she will become depressed and self-destructive. Her response to the conflicts in her family illustrate this. Another example occurred during one of her hospitalizations. Her doctor made a mistake and discontinued some pain medication she was taking for her arthritis. Ethel felt this was wrong and was very upset. Her response was to refuse to eat or take any medication until the error was remedied. Ethel is not without her own authority but she does not seem able to express it directly.

The theologian Dorothee Soelle has described a sequence of stages in response to suffering, beginning with muteness, moving to lament, and finally to action in solidarity with others.[3] Ethel's response to the suffering in her life has taken the form of self-destructive muteness or helpless lament. It is not uncommon for her to tell the story of what has happened to her in a fashion that communicates, "This is what they did to me. Isn't it terrible."

She seems less able to move from complaint or lament to negotiation or effective problem solving.[4]

There are also times when things are going well in Ethel's life—when she has a considerable measure of inner authority, which she brings into dialogue and relationship with others. When she was in the hospital and feeling better, she herself would pray on behalf of the chaplain, other staff, and her family. In several of her hospitalizations she was also selected by the other patients to be the chairperson of the unit's community meetings.

The extensive nature of this spiritual assessment of Ethel makes it important to develop a **spiritual assessment summary**. This is my spiritual assessment summary of Ethel.

> The death of her husband of nearly forty years and additional medical and family crises have made the past three years a period of great stress for Ethel. Overall she has coped remarkably well with these problems. However, Ethel's meaning in life depends heavily on her role and relationships in her immediate family. Her husband's death and conflicts with her daughter and granddaughter seriously threatened this base of meaning and spiritual well-being, resulting in periods of depression and suicidal thoughts requiring hospitalization. The absence of her son did not seem to be painful to Ethel, but it could be a factor in her depression. The birth of her new great-grandson has brought new meaning and satisfaction back into her life. Hopefully this period of relative stability and well-being will continue. It could be threatened by new conflicts in the family, or when the baby gets older and more assertive, or if Veronica should move away.
>
> Ethel's sense of closeness to God appears to fluctuate with the level of harmony in her family life. In the past she has been quite active in her local church, but she has not been very involved there for several years and shows little interest in renewing that activity. However, she has a good relationship with the church's pastor, and his crisis intervention and sustaining interest and care mean a great deal to her. It appears that her group of professional medical helpers is becoming community to her.

In addition to my spiritual assessment of Ethel, it is important to include Ethel's **spiritual self-assessment**. At this point Ethel describes herself as happy and fulfilled. She derives great pleasure from being a great-grandmother, watching her great-grandson grow and helping to take care of him. When we talk she always tells me the latest news about the baby. I think Ethel would say that this happiness is a gift from God.

Ethel also takes some pride in having come through the ordeal of her grief, depression, and hospitalizations. She is aware that her desire to get well again and her willingness to follow the treatment plan recommended to her were key factors in her recovery. At the same time as she takes credit for what she accomplished, she is thankful toward all those who helped her: physicians, nurses, pastor, and friends. Her gratitude is also directed toward God, who helped make it all possible.

I think Ethel would say she does not have any pressing spiritual needs at present. She would be hopeful that her granddaughter and great-grandson stay well and that she herself stays well. The pastor's periodic calls to see how she is doing reassures her, as do her occasional phone calls to me. Knowing that she can call and get help if she should need it also means a lot to her.

The main purpose of spiritual assessment is to guide our pastoral care. What should be our **pastoral care plan** for ministry with Ethel? I will address this question from the perspective of her parish pastor and from the perspective of the chaplain.

I think that Ethel's spiritual self-assessment is correct. She is doing well now, and I do not think much special pastoral care is called for. Pastor Smith is maintaining a supportive pastoral relationship with Ethel, and that is a central point in the pastoral care plan. A monthly visit or phone call would provide a time to hear the latest news about the baby and celebrate that blessing with Ethel. The conversation could focus on any special concerns Ethel might have about her family or her health. It would be good to use the visits as a time to keep Ethel up-to-date about news from the church and any members with whom she is close. Periodically the pastor could talk with Ethel about attending worship and encourage her to feel welcome to join in church activities. Of course, the pastor can also share prayer with her, bringing before God the joys and concerns they have discussed.

In his pastoral visits the pastor could also think about spending some time with Veronica and her husband. Although this spiritual assessment has focused on Ethel, it is important not to lose sight of the needs of other members of her family, including this young couple, their relationship, and how they are handling the responsibility and stress of parenthood. I would invite them to participate in the life of the church in whatever way they were comfortable, including membership and the baptism of Benjamin. The pastor could also encourage them to consider the fellowship programs that try to connect the young families in the church and the religious education programs for children when their baby is older.

Hopefully this supportive pastoral relationship would meet Ethel's spiritual needs for many months to come. Yet it is also important to be ready to respond in case Ethel experiences another period of stress or crisis, perhaps related to her health or to conflict in the family.

From my perspective as the hospital chaplain, my pastoral care plan for the future focuses on being available and supportive. Ethel has developed a pattern of calling every four to six weeks. Sometimes the calls are related to news about her latest doctor's appointment, but sometimes they are simply to keep us in touch. I do not think that more is required right now, but again, as with the pastor, it seems important to be available in case another crisis emerges.

In the context of this discussion of the pastoral care plans for future ministry with Ethel, I would like to review the care I provided over the two-year period being considered here, noting in particular how the issues of authority and direction were handled in my work with her. During Ethel's first hospitalization my care was primarily supportive. I listened with empathy to Ethel's story about Ed's death and about her fears for the future. I offered prayers for her recovery from depression and the stabilization of her diabetes as well as for her hopes to return home. I also took something of an advocacy role and helped link the pastor and his resources for Ethel's discharge with the treatment team. In the months after discharge, Ethel kept in touch with me by phone, or we arranged to visit when she was at the hospital for a doctor's visit. Things were basically going well during those months, and my ministry was encouraging and supportive. I see all of this as care that was consistent with Ethel's wishes, and in retrospect I think it was the appropriate care to provide.

When Veronica became pregnant, Ethel called to ask for help with a referral for prenatal care. She also shared her distress about all the conflicts in the family. In the conversations we had during the weeks before she was hospitalized, and after she was in the hospital, in addition to being empathic I also began to give Ethel some advice she was not asking for. I began to stress that she could not solve Veronica's problems for her and that Ethel needed to have some interests and activities aside from her involvement with Veronica. A theme in this hospitalization was Ethel's struggle to feel good about herself. I emphasized my belief that she was a person of value in my eyes and in God's eyes, and that appropriate care for herself would include activities that she valued, such as volunteer work in a local community agency. Ethel appreciated the supportive pastoral care I provided at this time, but she was resistant when I went beyond that. Ethel resisted my advice about the need to disengage from Veronica's life and the related need for family therapy. She also resisted my suggestions that she develop interests and activities aside from her family.

By what authority did I make these suggestions? They stemmed from my observations about Ethel and conversation with others on the team about what was contributing to her distress and what might relieve it. I shared with Ethel my observations and the advice I drew from them. She was able to see some wisdom in the ideas, but it was hard for her to embrace them. At the time of her discharge there were recommendations for Ethel to follow up with both family therapy and new activities for herself. She made some efforts to follow through with these, but her basic lack of interest and some complications in each area meant that nothing really came of these suggestions. They had not been based on Ethel's sense of what was important, and so she did not pursue them.

The same may be said for Ethel's third hospitalization. With the team, I had suggested that Ethel should seek some pastoral counseling after she was discharged, both for support at times of any future family conflict and to help her feel some improvement in her sense of self-worth. Again, this was a recommendation that did not originate with Ethel, and she did not follow through with it, especially after the baby was born a few weeks later.

Using the framework of assessment, I would say that in Ethel's second and third hospitalizations she and I had differing assessments of the causes of her distress and what might be done to address it. In each case I presented my recommendations to her, she was hesitant about them, I argued the case for my recommendations, and Ethel appeared to agree. But since she had not really changed her mind, she did not act on these recommendations.

I take two lessons from this. The first is that spiritual assessment must be more than the caregiver's assessment of the situation. It must also include attention to the explicit or implicit self-assessment of the person for whom we are caring. To say this is actually to come back to a longstanding principle in pastoral care, that we can only begin where the partner in the pastoral relationship is, both for practical and ethical reasons.

The second lesson I take from this experience is that the process of spiritual assessment, especially using a model such as the 7×7, will often provide us with extensive information about people, about how they have come to be who they are, and what their possibilities for the future might include. In my experience, the next steps of those we minister to are often more modest than our assessments have envisioned. In situations such as this, our spiritual assessment provides us with a broad understanding of the person and the situation as well as the information necessary to respond to that person's more immediate pastoral needs.

I mentioned at the start of this chapter that I have known Ethel for more than five years. This spiritual assessment of Ethel has been limited to the first two years of our relationship. Before bringing this chapter to a close, I would like to tell you how things are going for Ethel.

In the three years since the last hospitalization discussed here, Ethel has not had any further episodes of depression or suicidal thinking nor any further psychiatric hospitalizations. Veronica and her husband had another baby about two years later. Ethel seems to enjoy being part of this busy household. She has been in the hospital for several surgeries; and in one case it took many weeks for the incision to heal, and she went through a long ordeal. Despite this, her mood remained positive, a fact in which she justifiably took some pride. There have been no major family upsets, and in fact there appears to be more stable harmony now than previously. She continues to have a warm relationship with Pastor Smith but has not become active in church or any pursuits outside her home. I hope that everything continues to go well for her and her growing family.

NOTES

1. One reader of this case has raised questions about whether the diagnosis of Ethel as having a borderline personality disorder is accurate. This reader saw in Ethel a higher level of functioning, in her marriage, for example, than is usually the case in people with severe borderline personality disorder.

2. Jared D. Kass, "Contributions of Religious Experience to Psychological and Physical Well-Being: Research Evidence and an Explanatory Model," *The Care Giver Journal* 8, 4 (1992): 4–11.

3. Soelle, *Suffering*.

4. Ethel's case may be an excellent illustration of the consequences of what Old Testament scholar Walter Brueggemann has called the costly loss of lament. Brueggemann asserts that the lament Psalms represent a form of protest that have important implications for both ego strength and social justice. He further states that the spirit they represent has been lost and replaced by civility and docility. "In that loss we may unwittingly endorse a false self that can take no initiative toward an omnipotent God. We may also unwittingly endorse unjust systems about which no questions can be properly raised. . . . Both *psychological inauthenticity and social immobility* may be derived from the loss of these texts." (67, emphasis in the original). I consider this an excellent assessment of Ethel's spiritual situation. See Walter Brueggemann, "The Costly Loss of Lament," *Journal for the Study of the Old Testament* 36 (1986): 57–71. On the implications of the lament Psalms for pastoral care, see George B. Zornow, "Recovering the Forgotten Spirituality of Lamentation," *The Care Giver Journal* 7, 1 (1990): 104–17.

Chapter 5

BOB FINDS HOPE

For several years our pastoral care department had a monthly case conference that focused on the spiritual assessment of people with HIV infection or AIDS. The participants in the conference were pastoral caregivers, staff, and students from several different HIV/AIDS ministries in Chicago. Our overall aim was to refine our understanding of the spiritual needs of people with this disease.

Bob was one of the cases we discussed early in this project. Chaplain Angelica, a resident in our training program, brought his case to the group in part because she felt frustrated in her efforts to help him. I hope that looking at this case will illustrate how our model for spiritual assessment can be used for problem solving in the midst of a caregiving relationship.

The Case

Background and Referral

Bob, a gay, white male in his midforties, had end-stage AIDS at the time of our case conference. He had been diagnosed with HIV infection three and a half years earlier.

Angelica met Bob during his first hospitalization here. He'd had several hospitalizations since his diagnosis prior to their meeting. Bob had not requested a chaplain's visit, and the nursing staff had not made a specific referral to see him. Angelica became acquainted with Bob on her routine visits to all new patients in her units.

Angelica had known Bob for nine months at the time of our case conference. This was his fifth hospitalization since they had met. This hospitalization had been precipitated by uncontrolled high fever. Since his first hospitalization Bob had suffered with many of the symptoms associated with AIDS, including pneumocystis pneumonia, thrush, cytomegalovirus (CMV) retinitis, and staph infections.

I will present this case by first describing the difficulties Chaplain Angelica was experiencing in her ministry with Bob, and then reviewing the history of her relationship with him and more of the information about his case.

Chaplain Angelica's Impasse

Bob had been in the hospital for four weeks at the time of the case conference. He had been very ill when he was first admitted. Both Bob and his partner, Ted, were afraid Bob was dying. In the first few days of this hospitalization, the staff was also quite concerned. However, they soon felt Bob's condition had improved and that he was no longer in danger of imminent death.

As Bob's condition stabilized and improved, he shared with Chaplain Angelica that he felt very bored. He complained there was nothing for him to do to pass the time. He was interested only in a few programs on television, and he said he did not enjoy watching them because he had problems with his eyesight, one of the complications of his illness.

In the previous hospitalization Chaplain Angelica had learned of Bob's interest in art. She also knew that the hospital's volunteer department could supply materials for some simple art projects. She suggested this to Bob and he seemed interested. She gave Bob the number of the volunteer office so he could call it.

Several days later Bob was still complaining to Angelica about being bored. She asked if he had called the volunteers. He said that he had not, but that he planned to call them the next day. Several days later he still had not called, and he was still complaining about being bored. Angelica told him that she would call, and he said that was fine.

The next day when Angelica visited, Bob was pleased and animated as he spoke of the volunteer's visit and the two art projects he had selected to work on. He said he planned to work on them later. Bob never worked on the projects. In subsequent days he said he didn't have the energy for them. He thought he might work on them at home after he was discharged. He also continued to complain about being bored.

As Angelica described her relationship with Bob, she said she felt "mired down." He spent a lot of his time with her complaining. Angelica felt that Bob could have done something to change the situations he was unhappy with, and they would often discuss his options. Angelica felt it was best for Bob if he tried to change things himself rather than having her or someone else make changes for him. But Bob never followed up on those conversations and continued to complain.

Let's look back at the history of Chaplain Angelica's relationship with Bob and what he shared with her about himself. Hopefully this will help us understand him better and Chaplain Angelica's ministry with him. I will begin by reviewing the sequence of his hospitalizations, beginning with the one where they met.

First Hospitalization.   Bob was in the hospital for about a week during the time he and Angelica became acquainted. He never explicitly asked for the chaplain's help with any problem or directly expressed any need. However, he shared a lot about himself with Angelica and welcomed her visits. He told Angelica that as a child other children teased him harshly because of his slight build and glasses. He was not athletic and had very few friends among his peers. He told the chaplain these experiences led him to have very low self-esteem and to feel worthless.

The theme of feeling worthless stood out as Bob shared himself with Angelica. He said that all his life he had felt worthless. He said this feeling began in his childhood and had been compounded by being gay. He said that Ted was the only person in his life who had been able to begin to teach him to love himself. At the same time, he said he was not worthy of Ted, and he would frequently tell Angelica that he was not worthy of her and was taking too much of her time. Bob had met Ted about ten years before. At the time, Bob lived in Wisconsin near his family and Ted lived in Chicago. After about five years Bob moved to Chicago to live with Ted.

Bob shared that he had been raised in a small town. He had two sisters, one older and one younger than himself, and one younger brother. He said his parents were divorced and his dad had remarried. His mother, whom he described as a suspicious and antisocial person, was quite ill herself. She neglected her health and lived with a cousin who did her best to care for her. Bob hadn't had much contact with her. Bob described his relationship with his dad as OK. Since his remarriage his dad had developed a strong interest in religion, which made Bob uncomfortable.

Bob's older sister had moved away and had little contact with the rest of the family. He felt he had a good relationship and could talk freely with his younger sister, who like his brother, still lived in the town they were raised in. Bob said he did not get along with his younger brother, whom he described as homophobic. Bob said his family didn't like Ted but that they were relieved that Ted was there to care for Bob since "they live in fear that I will turn up on their doorstep."

Bob was raised in the Roman Catholic church but quit attending when he was a teenager. He was a high school graduate and was employed in factory work. Because of his illness he had been on disability and hadn't worked for more than a year. He had few friends beside Ted and few activities that interested him. After he was diagnosed as HIV+, he became involved with an AIDS awareness education group in the gay community. He had not been active with them since his first hospitalization.

As he talked about his life that week, Bob shared with the chaplain that things were different for him in the hospital than elsewhere. In the hospital he felt comfortable, he felt cared for. He felt people were willing to listen to him, unlike what he said happened in other places in his life. As he described other relationships in his life, Bob's pattern of complaining began to emerge. He had serious criticisms regarding all of the people in his life whom he mentioned, even Ted. And while he said he felt cared for in the hospital, he also complained about his relationships with people there.

Chaplain Angelica was moved by the depth of Bob's feelings of unworthiness. Although he made no explicit request for pastoral care from her, she decided to continue to visit him whenever he was in the hospital. She hoped that by establishing a relationship with him in which he would feel accepted by her and by treating him as a person who was valuable to her she would be able to help him accept himself more and feel more self-worth.

Angelica's goals with Bob were characteristic of her approach to pastoral care. They in fact characterize much of modern pastoral care, which has been strongly influenced by the client-centered model of psychotherapy. Explicit discussion of religious issues and religious rituals are often a small part of this style of pastoral care. However, in this first hospitalization, Chaplain Angelica asked Bob if she could pray with him. He consented but then interrupted her and changed the subject in the midst of her prayer. She didn't comment on that, but when it happened a second time, she decided not to pray with him. Instead as she ended her visits with Bob she would share with him the focus of her prayer for him that day. She was uncertain if Bob's interruptions were his way of saying he was uncomfortable with her prayers, or if he simply never had anyone pray with him before and was unfamiliar with how to act in that situation.

Second Hospitalization. Bob's second hospitalization came about two and a half months after the first and lasted just over a week. Many of the things that Bob talked about during this hospitalization were similar to those from the previous hospitalization.

Now his complaints about the way other people treated him were focused on Irene, Ted's sister. In recent months when Bob had become less able to care for himself at home, she would come and spend the day helping to care for him while Ted was at work. A program for AIDS patients paid for in-home caregivers like Irene. Bob had tried several other caregivers, and while Irene was better than the other workers, Bob spent a lot of time complaining about her. He said she never followed his directions when he asked her to do something for him. If he asked her to make him something to eat, for example, she would prepare something for him but it would not be what he had requested. Bob told Angelica that he thought Irene really didn't like him and that her behavior was her way of getting back at him.

Angelica told the case conference she wasn't sure what was happening. From his descriptions it sounded as though Irene was not as careful in responding to Bob's requests as she might be. But at the same time, Bob was similarly critical of almost everyone, including those who did appear to be more attentive to his needs and wishes.

One day Bob told Chaplain Angelica about an incident in which he had lost his temper and yelled at Irene. As he told the story, he was very self-critical, saying he knew he should not have behaved that way toward Irene. Angelica interjected that it appeared Bob was being pretty harsh on himself and wondered if he might be more self-forgiving. This led to some discussion about how no one is perfect and how all people fall short of their ideals. Bob said, "I'll have to think about that," and was shortly complaining about another incident with Irene.

Third Hospitalization. Bob was hospitalized for a third time about two months later. The hospitalization lasted less than a week. One day when he was feeling very ill, he told Chaplain Angelica that he thought he would die the next time he was hospitalized. This was the first time he had mentioned his death to the chaplain. They did not discuss it further during this hospitalization.

However, in their conversation the theme of disappointment with others and forgiveness did reemerge. It focused around Bob's jealousy over Ted's relationship with a friend of theirs, Jack. Jack was a frequent weekend guest at Ted and Bob's. Bob denied that he was jealous of the time Ted spent with Jack, saying he was simply concerned about the burden of this extra hospitality when he wasn't feeling well. He never spoke directly to Jack about his concern but nagged Ted until Ted told Jack not to visit anymore.

Bob felt bad after Ted did that and called Jack to say he was welcome, but on a less frequent basis. Shortly after that Ted sent Bob some flowers in the hospital. When Chaplain Angelica remarked on the lovely flowers, Bob said with obvious excitement that Ted had sent them. Then his tone and expression changed and he remarked that they were probably meant as a reward for Bob's apology to Jack. Bob checked himself as he said this, realizing that it was at least equally as likely that Ted's only reason for sending the flowers was to express his love and to cheer Bob up.

Fourth Hospitalization. Bob was hospitalized again about a month later for over a week. His general condition was deteriorating. By this time he was taking a large number of different medications, and many of them had side effects that made him feel very sick. On his own he had stopped taking some of them. He said he was tired of being sick, that he was ready to die, and that he didn't want to take any more pills.

Bob's physician met with him. He told Bob that if he adjusted some of the medication, he was sure that Bob would feel better. Bob told Angelica the doctor had told him, "Now listen to me. I'll tell you when you can give up." Bob took the medications that were being prescribed and began to feel better and was soon discharged.

Fifth Hospitalization.   Six weeks later Bob needed to be in the hospital again, this time for more than five weeks. Bob's condition was getting worse. This time both Bob and Ted felt that he was near death, and the staff shared this concern for the first few days. Bob responded to the treatment that was initiated and soon was more stable. He continued to have unpredictable episodes of high fever, however, which set back several discharge plans. He also had several episodes of awakening at night and being extremely anxious and unable to get back to sleep. During these episodes he called Ted, who came to the hospital to be with him. After Ted arrived Bob was less anxious and eventually able to return to sleep.

There were some significant changes in Bob's religious practices during this hospitalization. In the first few days, when Bob's condition was critical, Ted called Bob's family to tell them what was happening. Even though Bob soon was more stable, Bob's father, stepmother, younger sister, and brother came to visit. During the visit Bob's father repeated an admonition he had shared with Bob on other occasions. He told his son that he needed to renounce his homosexuality, his relationship with Ted, and "get right with God." The family visit lasted several hours. Chaplain Angelica met several members of the family but didn't have any sustained conversation with them. She thought they appeared tense. Bob told Angelica he had been glad to see his family but was even happier to see them go.

Some time after his family's visit, Bob shared with Angelica that he had discussed some of his funeral plans with Ted. He said that after his death he wanted his body to be cremated and his ashes scattered over a lake. His family, however, wanted his ashes to be buried in the family plot. Bob told Angelica, "They're my family. I really should do what they want. Ted has all these memories of me, and they don't have anything."

Not long after his family's visit, Bob asked Chaplain Angelica if he could receive Holy Communion daily. Angelica said that it definitely was possible. Because it is customary for many Roman Catholics who have not recently participated in the sacraments of the church to receive the sacrament of reconciliation before receiving communion, Angelica asked Bob if he wanted to see the priest for the sacrament of reconciliation. Bob said no, but that he would like to receive communion. Later that day Angelica gave communion to Bob.

Later she asked Bob what receiving the sacrament meant to him. He said that his father's comment had made him think about getting spiritually ready to die. He wondered if he was receiving the sacrament for himself or in order to please his father. It was really for himself, he decided. He said that receiving the sacrament gave him a sense of peace and helped him to feel closer to God. He said the Eucharist had to do with salvation, not that he was automatically saved because he was receiving it, but it made him feel easier about the possibility of salvation. "It's a comfort to take a little bit of the Lord," Bob concluded.

Angelica made a referral for Bob to receive daily communion from the volunteer eucharistic ministers who assist the department. She could have continued to serve him herself, but she thought he would appreciate the contact with other visitors. This proved to be a good assessment. Bob commented that he enjoyed their visits, and one volunteer who had served him on a number of occasions remarked about how gracious Bob was and how much she enjoyed visiting with him. Later in this hospitalization Bob mentioned to his sister that he had begun to receive the sacrament. She told their father. Bob said his sister reported that his father was happy that he had begun to receive communion. As Bob's condition finally stabilized and plans were made for his discharge, Ted's mother, who lives near Bob and Ted, made arrangements with her parish for Bob to continue to receive communion while he was at home.

About the time that Bob began to receive communion, he also received a card from a relative, one with a simple prayer in it, similar to the Serenity Prayer, and a note saying that Bob should recite the prayer daily. Bob placed the card near his bed and told Angelica that he was reciting it each day. As they talked, Bob said he had begun to think about how he had previously rejected God, but now he had begun to hope that God would accept him as he was.

In another conversation, Bob told Angelica that he had called his sister. He said he wanted her to do him a favor and make an appointment for lunch with one of Bob's boyhood friends. He asked his sister to tell the friend that Bob was gay and that he had AIDS. Bob told Angelica that he didn't want to die without his friend knowing this about him, but that he was afraid to tell his friend directly.

Near the end of this hospitalization the health care team organized a discharge planning conference. Ted was invited and attended. Bob was also invited but asked that Ted represent him and communicate to him later what was discussed. This was the first time Angelica met Ted. She sensed that he was very tired and that caring for Bob was beginning to overwhelm him. She also saw that he preferred to cope by minimizing his own needs and stress and finding ways to do as much for Bob as he could.

The team suggested that Ted and Bob consider contacting a local hospice to get additional support for caring for Bob after he was discharged. Ted thought that seemed like a good idea. However, when this hospitalization came to an end, Ted and Bob elected to continue aggressive therapy where it was available and to use the home health nursing agency they had previously used.

Sixth Hospitalization. About a week and a half after this discharge, Bob became very sick and was hospitalized for about ten days. He told Chaplain

Angelica that he was sure that he would recover this time, and he did. He said it wasn't yet time to get involved with the hospice. He told Angelica that he thought Ted was getting tired of taking care of him and that Ted was arguing in favor of a hospice and palliative care because he hoped Bob would die sooner.

Chaplain Angelica's year of training was coming to an end as Bob was being discharged. Before he left she told him that she would be leaving soon. They said good-bye to each other. Bob told her that she had been helpful to him and that he appreciated her care very much. She told Bob that it had meant a great deal to her to have known him and that she would keep him in her prayers. She reminded Bob that if he had to come back to the hospital again, he or Ted could ask the nurses to call for a chaplain.

Assessment

When I think about this case I realize there are times when I don't like Bob. His constant complaining and his suspicion and criticism of people, especially people who seem to be doing their best to help him, make me angry. I also feel sad and sorry for him when I think about the deprived and hostile environment he grew up in. I don't like his judgmental father or homophobic brother. I like Ted and all that he does to care for Bob. I really like Chaplain Angelica and her work with Bob. Her faithful and accepting presence and care reflect the best in our work. This is a case that stirs up a lot of feelings for me.

As I have noted, there was no explicit **referral** for pastoral care in this case. Chaplain Angelica met Bob in the course of her routine visits with all new patients. While Bob never explicitly asked the chaplain for any help, he always greeted her warmly when she visited and readily shared his concerns with her. His description of low self-worth in his early conversations with the chaplain led her to provide ongoing pastoral care. Although the chaplain's initial visit in this case did not stem from a referral, on numerous occasions during his hospitalizations the staff asked Angelica to visit Bob, especially when he was having a particularly bad day or when they needed someone to share the work of listening to his latest complaints.

Holistic Assessment

As we have in the other cases, we begin our multidisciplinary assessment by reviewing Bob's **medical condition**. There are many details to Bob's symptoms and treatment, but it is not necessary to review all of them here. He has AIDS, and the disease has progressed to a point commonly referred to as end-stage AIDS. At the time of his fifth and sixth hospitalizations, his condition was grave and his prognosis quite poor. He has pain and feels weak almost constantly. He spends almost all of his time in bed. Frequently he runs a high fever. His eyesight has been impaired. He does not sleep well and is often nauseous and short of breath. Some of the medications he takes have side effects that make him feel worse. He is still able to perform most of the activities of daily living. On most days he is able to bathe and dress himself if he has some assistance. He does not appear to be suffering any of the cognitive impairment that is often seen in AIDS patients at this stage of the illness. To the statement "I'm content with the quality of my life right now" on the hospital's research forms, Bob responded, "Not at all."

How can we describe Bob from a **psychological perspective?** Bob has no known history of psychiatric illness or treatment prior to or since his diagnosis with AIDS. He describes himself as a person with a very low sense of self-worth, a lifelong problem. His internalized homophobia, sharing society's view of gay people as deviant, appears to be a factor in his problem with self-acceptance.

Bob appears to have trouble trusting other people and is often suspicious of their motives. He frequently communicates his wishes in a passive-aggressive way, as he did in nagging Ted about the time he was spending with Jack. One of the nurses told Angelica that Bob always saw the "glass-half-empty" side of life. Bob said that in contrast to the rest of his life, he felt that the people in the hospital listened to him, and he felt comfortable and cared for while there.

From our observations of his behavior and comments, I would suggest that, among other things, Bob is struggling with feelings about dependency, a struggle he is probably not conscious of. His wishes to have someone to take care of him likely predate his illness, but they become more significant as he feels sicker and weaker. With the exception of Ted, there appears to have been no one in his life whom Bob could trust to care for him. Consequently he is suspicious and critical of the people who do care for him, and he is highly indirect in expressing his needs. Being in the hospital is an important exception. Here it is OK to need help and be taken care of, and the staff does an excellent job of accepting Bob and doing all they can to meet his needs.

What are the important features of Bob's case from a **family systems perspective?** Bob's family of election, his relationship with Ted, appears to be basically healthy. They have known each other for more than ten years and have lived together for about half of that time. The relationship continues to be positive and supportive even in the face of the severe stresses caused by Bob's illness. Ted's family appears to be accepting of both him and Bob.

Bob's family, by contrast, avoids the couple and is quite judgmental regarding them. Bob's relationship with his family of origin is filled with problems. His childhood seems to have been marked by neglect and rejection. Consistent with this history, he senses that now that he has AIDS they want no part of caring for him.

Bob has little relationship with his mother, who is physically and psychologically ill. He has little contact with his father and siblings but seems to be somewhat more invested in those relationships, at least as far as his father and younger sister are concerned. Both his father and brother have a condemning attitude toward Bob because of his homosexuality. Chaplain Angelica described his relationship with his father as very ambivalent, Bob both loving him and being angry with him.

There are indications that since Bob's fifth hospitalization and the family's visit, some rapprochement is occurring. I see signs of this in Bob's willingness to let his family bury his ashes in the family plot and in his positive response to the news that his father is pleased to know he is receiving communion.

When we review Bob's case from a **psychosocial perspective** we note that he was born and raised in a small town where most of his family still live. He is a high school graduate and has worked in various semiskilled manufacturing jobs. He has been on disability for several years. His health care expenses are being covered by Medicaid. Bob lives with Ted in a home that is near Ted's family, who provide some assistance with caring for Bob.

Bob has few friendships. His leisure interests have included art and cooking. His illness has made it difficult for him to continue with either of these.

Bob's case is somewhat difficult to assess from the **ethnic, racial, and cultural perspective**. He is a white, gay male, born and raised in the Midwest. From Chaplain Angelica's report, I do not get a sense that important aspects of Bob's identity or interests are associated with his racial or ethnic origin. Nor does it appear that he is strongly identified with any aspects of the city's gay community and its cultural interests and activities. It is possible that there are important ways in which Bob identifies with the gay community and they simply have not come up in his sharing with the chaplain.

What important considerations from the **societal issues perspective** can we see in Bob's case? Unfortunately Bob's case is a good illustration of how larger cultural and social dynamics cause or contribute to an individual's suffering. For Bob this is evident in the condemning attitude toward his homosexuality that he has experienced from his family, church, and community. Many AIDS patients are unable to get good medical care and lack personal support to assist them when they are ill. Fortunately that is not the case for Bob. He has access to excellent medical care and has sufficient personal support from Ted and some members of Ted's family.

Spiritual Assessment

For Bob I'd like to change the order of the seven spiritual dimensions. No strong reason exists for staying with the sequence as it was given earlier. The order of the outline can be revised as needed to suit the specifics of a given case.

Because there was a significant change in Bob's **rituals and practices** in the course of his fifth hospitalization, my spiritual assessment of him will begin with this dimension. At the beginning of Chaplain Angelica's relationship with Bob, he did not appear to have any significant religious or non-religious rituals or practices that gave his life meaning, expressed his values, or gave him comfort and peace. In fact Angelica had the impression that when she prayed with him, he was either uncomfortable with this practice or quite unfamiliar with it.

Yet I might argue that Bob's complaining functions like a litany. It is as if his daily prayer went something like, "O Lord, no one knows how unhappy I am. I am surrounded by people who don't listen to me and who don't seem to care," and he would proceed to enumerate his grievance at length. Yet two characteristics of a litany are absent from Bob's version of it. Bob's lament is not consciously addressed to God. It's addressed to anyone who will stop and listen. But because it is a grating litany, most people are put off by it. Consequently there is no community to recite the litany with Bob, no community that identifies with his suffering.

An important change took place in Bob's fifth hospitalization, after his visit with his father. He asked if he could begin to receive communion on a daily basis, and he also began to recite a prayer each day. He said it gave him a sense of peace "to take a bit of the Lord." The two things that had been missing in Bob's complaining litany were now present. For Bob, as for many of us, God is more immediately present in the sacrament than in almost any other way we can encounter God. Additionally, the ritual is a highly communal activity. Community begins with the communion minister who brings Bob the sacrament, but it extends to include all those who are also gathered at the Lord's table with Bob, to be fed in body and spirit. As I continue with the spiritual assessment, I will look at this change from other spiritual perspectives.

What can be said about the **beliefs and meaning** in Bob's life? Angelica never had a conversation with Bob about what gave his life meaning. But as we listen to what he shared and observe his behavior, it seems evident that his relationship with Ted is the most important thing in his life. If that were taken from him, I think he would feel there was no other meaning or purpose in his life.

What can we say about beliefs that are important to Bob, that guide him or give him meaning? Until his fifth hospitalization I would have said I was not aware of any beliefs that were important for him. After his family's visit, when he asked to receive communion, it appeared that a number of beliefs were important to him. These all seem to be beliefs associated with the Roman Catholic faith of his childhood, including belief in the importance of the sacraments and prayer. Bob also mentioned belief in salvation, and in a new understanding of God as accepting him. He said he was not yet sure if he was saved.

Something significant appears to have happened in the course of Bob's fifth hospitalization which we can look at further as we consider the dimension of **courage and growth**. During that time Bob's **religious practices** changed, notably daily holy communion and the daily recitation of the prayer sent by his relative. His comment about his hope that God accepted him indicates that a significant change in his beliefs was taking place.

As I try to assess the dimension of **courage and growth,** I ask two questions: first, what caused the changes, and second, should the changes be evaluated as courage, growth, or something else? I think three factors need to be considered when we ask what caused the changes; his nearness to death, his father's visit, and Chaplain Angelica's ministry.

Bob was aware that his condition was getting worse and that his death might be near. Those who minister with terminally ill people find that death-bed conversions are far less common than is often supposed, but they do occur. Some research has found that terminally ill hospitalized adults scored higher on a spiritual perspective scale and were more likely to report changes toward increased spirituality than hospitalized adults who were not terminally ill or healthy adults from the community.[1] Was awareness of his own nearness to death a factor in Bob's changes in religious practices?

We need to consider the role his father's visit played in these changes. Bob's father had periodically admonished his son to get right with God, by which Bob understood him to mean to end his relationship with Ted and change from being homosexual. During his visit he apparently repeated this warning. After Bob had begun to receive communion, he wondered whether he was doing it to satisfy his father or for himself. Bob concluded that he was receiving communion for himself, but the fact that his father was pleased also was important to Bob. His father's visit seemed to have helped him take some concrete steps to prepare for his death.

The third factor that played a crucial role was Chaplain Angelica's ministry. The goal of her ministry with Bob had been to accept him as he was and to relate to him as a person of worth and value and by doing so to help him feel a greater sense of his worth and value. I think Bob's comment that he had begun to hope that God accepted him as he was, was made possible by his experience with a representative of God's acceptance, Chaplain Angelica. This crucial experience gave him hope and helped him take the step to request communion.

We still need to consider, however, whether this change should be called courage, growth, or regression. I raise the possibility that Bob's change represents regression because of the condemnation of homosexuality by most churches. This stance has made it difficult for gay men and lesbians to develop their spirituality while affirming their sexual orientation. For many this has meant distancing themselves from the church, as Bob did in his teen years. Some gay men and lesbians find ways to continue their spiritual development privately or through alternative spiritual communities.[2] But, like Bob, many simply try to avoid the issue. Yet, it remains an unfinished piece of business, stuck at the point where they felt condemned and when they ended their involvement with the church.

We might wonder whether Bob's sudden return to the religion of his childhood was a regressive response to anxiety about his death and an effort to appease both his earthly and heavenly fathers.[3] However, his later comment that he no longer rejected God but hoped God accepted him as he was indicates that his change is differentiated from his father's anxiety and judgmental faith. In the last weeks of the fifth hospitalization and in the sixth hospitalization, Chaplain Angelica also noticed a small decrease in the number of complaints and Bob's references to his low self-worth. These changes lend support to the assessment that Bob's increased religious practices represent growth and not regression.

I prefer to describe what we see in Bob as spiritual growth rather than courage. As I said in chapter 3, I use the term *courage* to refer to the process of living through times of profound doubt about fundamental religious beliefs. It does not appear to me that Bob has been through such a change. Rather it seems that he is separating himself from the religious teachings of the church and family of his childhood and exploring what it means to come to his own understanding of and relationship with God. Using John Westerhoff's framework, Bob had begun to move from affiliative faith to searching faith.[4]

When we look at the possibility that Bob is beginning to develop some religious beliefs independent of those he received from his church and family, we have also begun to look at the dimension of **authority and guidance** in this case. The first impression one gets about Bob's level of inner authority is that it is very low. The extent of his complaining behavior gives the impression that he is helpless and frequently victimized.

When Chaplain Angelica presented his case to the spiritual assessment study group, she sensed that Bob was able to do more than he tried to do. He had enough inner authority and sense of direction to know what he wanted and to be critical when he didn't get it, but he lacked the ability to take more direct initiative on his own behalf. When we look at the case from this perspective, it is also interesting to remember that Bob never asked Angelica for help or advice. In the face of the many problems caused by his illness, he really was not at a loss for guidance or the authority to make decisions.

Nonetheless my impression is that Bob struggles with authority and that there are three dimensions to his struggle. First, Bob's sense of authority is fragile. He talks as if he is sure of what he wants and needs, but it is more likely that he is unsure. His ideas and sense of direction for himself are vulnerable, so he talks as if he is more sure of himself than he is, or keeps his most vulnerable wishes extremely private.

Second, Bob has great difficulty trusting other people, especially when they are exercising authority and making decisions that will affect him. I assume that for much of his early life people in authority rejected or condemned Bob and that he expects that pattern to continue. I think this explains why he is suspicious and critical of Ted. This difficulty in trusting other people also means that Bob is likely to act unilaterally rather than to consult with others or test his ideas before proceeding to act on them. His decision to stop taking some of his medications is an example of this.

Third, I think Bob would like to be relieved of the burdens of making decisions for himself. He would like to be connected to someone who would take care of him and make decisions for him. His problem with trusting others makes it difficult for him to depend on helpful people who are available to him. His relationship with his physician seems to be a blessed exception, and Bob showed a great deal of trust and readily obeyed when he was told that his physician would let him know when the end was near. The quickness with which Bob accepted this order and the absence of any criticism about it points to the relief he found in being able to rely on his physician's authority.

When we look at the explicitly religious aspects of Bob's case, I think Bob's problem with trusting others' authority was a major factor in why he was so uncomfortable discussing his religious ideas or feelings with Chaplain Angelica. Her descriptions of his lack of eye contact during such conversations and his eagerness to change the subject make me think of an anxious schoolboy facing a harsh and rigid teacher in catechism class. From the number of times that Bob initiated some conversation about religion and from his obvious interest in maintaining the relationship with the chaplain, I judge that he had a wish to explore the religious aspect of his life. But it also seems that he was afraid of a negative response. Unfortunately his fear generally overpowered his desire for spiritual exploration, which limited the extent to which he and Angelica were able to discuss such issues.

In his religious life Bob exercised some positive authority in two places. The first came when he declined Chaplain Angelica's offer to contact the priest for the sacrament of reconciliation. It may be he didn't want to expose himself to the possibility of being judged by someone he didn't know—a wise move that I would generally support when the sympathies of the priest are not known, but in this case it was an unfounded anxiety. Perhaps Bob simply didn't feel a need for that ritual and felt no obligation to perform it. Either way, it strikes me as an important exercise of authority over his religious life.

The second instance of personal authority is seen in Bob's decision to receive communion not in order to appease a condemning Father but in order to grow closer to one he has begun to think of as accepting of him. This is a striking decision, and it points to another issue involving authority—the emergence of Bob's new relationship with authority. Bob accepted some of his father's authority. He did not hide from it or reject it completely. His father's admonition did carry the authority to cause Bob to think about his spiritual preparation for death. But unlike other times in his life, Bob now seemed able to bring his own authority into the picture. He began to consider a relationship with a God who accepts him as he is. This experience left a good taste in Bob's mouth, it gave him peace.

Bob said little to Chaplain Angelica that would enable us to assess the dimension of **vocation and consequences** in his life. However, his sense of duty to people with whom he has significant relationships stands out as we observe him and listen to his story. This is consistent with our assessment that the sense of meaning in his life comes through relationships, specifically his relationship with Ted. Bob is faithful in that relationship and repented when he was unreasonable about Ted's friendship with Jack. Bob also seems to feel some obligation to please his family, and especially his father, his hostile attitude toward Bob notwithstanding. This is seen in Bob's willingness to have his ashes buried in the family plot and in his response to knowing his father was pleased that he started receiving communion. Finally, concern about his boyhood friend is evident in Bob's request that his sister inform him about Bob's sexual orientation and illness.

What can we see when we look at the dimension of **experience and emotion** in Bob's case? Some counselors suggest that the homophobia and oppression that gay men experience is an experience of the demonic. I think that may be true. From the information we have, it appears that Bob has not had any direct experiences of the sacred.

What is the overall feeling that seems to describe Bob's spiritual life as we have been considering it? Bob described a feeling of peace that came as he began to receive communion. But the persistence of his pattern of complaining makes me reluctant to summarize the tone of his spiritual life with the term *peace*. The sense of being a helpless victim, or of being dissatisfied and complaining, seems far more pervasive. That was certainly true of Bob prior to his fifth hospitalization, and it remains true to a considerable extent even after his religious renewal. But Chaplain Angelica noticed some changes in the extent of his complaining. This is an area that may be in transition.

The image of Bob as a complaining victim points again to the problems of trust that are so significant in his life, and this leads us to review his case from the final spiritual dimension, **community**. I think this may be the dimension that provides the most important perspective to help us understand Bob and his spiritual life. Bob has little or no community, and it is hard for him to trust the community he does have. His lack of trust is understandable in light of the rejection and neglect to which he has been subjected by communities that should have been affirming—his family, church, and town.

With whom is Bob able to share the source of meaning in his life? Of course he shares it with Ted, but beyond that there do not appear to be any others who are aware of or celebrate the blessing that this couple is to each other. The absence of a community that can share in this important source of meaning for Bob is symbolized by the absence of a shared ritual marking their commitment, by the absence of a marriage ceremony.

What community shares Bob's ritual of complaining? None, of course. Some people tolerate it. Most people are put off by it. It is a ritual that has occupied a lot of Bob's time and energy, but it is one that has unfortunately undermined rather than built up community for him.

Bob seems to feel a sense of connectedness to his father and to his boyhood friend. He sends important messages to both of them through his sister, but he keeps his distance as well. Since he has begun receiving communion, his community has begun to widen, both practically, with the various communion ministers who visit him, and symbolically with all the faithful who join him at the Lord's table. The hospital is also a community where Bob feels comfortable. He feels listened to, understood, and accepted there.

Let me now offer a **summary spiritual assessment** as a way to bring all of this material together.

> Bob is a white, gay man in his midforties who has end-stage AIDS, which has necessitated more frequent hospitalizations for increasingly serious threats to his life. He has a positive and supportive relationship with his partner, Ted, with whom he has lived for the past four years. Bob's sense of meaning in life seems to be based primarily on his relationship with Ted. Additionally, this relationship constitutes virtually all of Bob's community. Aside from it, Bob appears to have few friends. Bob has some contact with his family, which provides little support, and his father and brother explicitly condemn him for his homosexuality.
>
> Bob spends a good deal of his time complaining about the ways other people have failed or mistreated him. Until recently this has been the dominant ritual activity in his life, expressing his conflicted wish to be cared for by others and his problems with trust and community. Although he rightly blames others for some gross mistreatment he has suffered, he has difficulty assuming appropriate responsibility for his life and trusting those who have proven themselves trustworthy in their relationships with him. Bob reports a lifelong sense of feeling worthless.
>
> Bob was raised as a Roman Catholic but stopped participating in the church as a teenager. Until recently Bob has not indicated any interest in religious ideas or practices. Several weeks ago Bob asked to receive communion on a daily basis and says that doing so gives him a sense of peace. This change was precipitated by a visit from his father, who admonished him to get right with God (that is, stop being homosexual) before he died. Bob sees his decision to receive the sacrament as something he's doing to prepare himself spiritually for death and not as an attempt to please his father. He said he has begun to hope

that, in contrast to his adolescent view, God accepts him as he is. This view represents a unique and positive expression of his sense of authority. These significant changes have been accompanied by a small decrease in his complaining about the way others treat him.

Now it is time to look at how the spiritual assessment of Bob helps us consult with Chaplain Angelica about her **pastoral care plan** for her ministry with him. I must confess that when I first listened to Angelica's presentation of his case, I wanted her to take more initiative with him in three different areas.

Regarding Bob's complaining and apparent helplessness, I sensed that Angelica had gotten caught up in dealing with a symptom and had been neglecting to look at the causes. Perhaps during one of Bob's complaint litanies about Ted or Irene, Angelica could have wondered with him whether his experiences of rejection as a child had made it hard for him to trust people. Such a question might have opened new avenues for them to explore together.

It also might have been helpful to inquire about any unfinished business Bob has with the church's teachings on homosexuality. As a way to explore this, Chaplain Angelica might have asked about his religious history and what was happening when he stopped attending church. Perhaps if the air could be cleared about that, his religious heritage could become a living resource for him as his life neared its end.

Finally I think it would have been useful if the chaplain had taken a bit more initiative earlier to suggest that she and Bob share some religious practices, such as prayer or communion or devotional readings. When such practices are carefully selected, they usually offer a great deal of support. Terminally ill patients who become progressively worse and no longer have the energy for in-depth conversations generally find these rituals supportive and comforting.

These are ways that I think Angelica could have augmented her pastoral care plan with Bob. But her plan of being present with Bob to provide him with an accepting relationship was just what he needed. It was a key to his finding peace and comfort, and not condemnation, in the renewal of his sacramental practices and relationship with God.

As Bob's health deteriorates I don't think it is appropriate for Angelica to try to address the dynamics that contribute to his complaining or helplessness. I would encourage her to avoid getting caught up in the specifics of that behavior and to see it instead as an expression of his difficulty in trusting and being in community with others.

In her case presentation Angelica did not talk about helping Bob die well as part of her care plan, but I think her ministry has played an important role in ensuring that this will happen. Whenever I am working with someone who is terminally ill, my goal always includes doing what I can to assure their safe conduct. By that I mean their passage through their sometimes difficult last days with as much dignity, comfort, and resolution of important relationships and issues as possible.[5]

As Angelica closed her ministry with Bob, I sensed that he was prepared to have as good a death as he possibly could. Bob told Angelica that one of the things he enjoyed doing was cooking, preparing tasteful, elegant dinners for himself and Ted. In the last few weeks that Angelica worked with him, it appeared that Bob had begun to imagine that the Lord had prepared a special banquet for him, that a table had been set at which he was awaited, a welcomed and honored guest. It was a feast of which he had begun to have a taste in his daily communion, and he found that it was satisfying his soul and giving him a new sense of peace.

This brings to an end our use of the 7 × 7 model to present examples of spiritual assessment in pastoral care. The next chapter describes some guidelines for evaluating the strengths and weaknesses of different models for spiritual assessment, including the 7 × 7 model.

NOTES

1. Pamela G. Reed, "Spirituality and Well-Being in Terminally Ill Hospitalized Adults," *Research in Nursing and Health* 10 (1987): 335–44.

2. A good discussion of spiritual development for gay men and lesbians is Craig O'Neill and Kathleen Ritter, *Coming out Within* (New York: HarperCollins, 1992).

3. Two studies appear to support the constructive nature of the tendency of gay men to differentiate from their childhood religion. Research by Franks and his colleagues found that gay men, with or without AIDS, were more likely to score lower on a death anxiety scale if they were no longer associated with the religion of their childhood. Further, death anxiety for those with AIDS was also lower when subjects reported having a spiritual belief system not associated with formal religion. Kent Franks, Donald I. Templer, Gordon G. Cappelletty, and Inge Kauffman, "Exploration of Death Anxiety as a Function of Religious Variables in Gay Men with and without AIDS," *Omega* 22, 1 (1900–91): 43–50.

In a study of hope and spiritual well-being in persons with AIDS, using Ellison's Spiritual Well-Being Scale to which I referred above, Carson and her colleagues found that higher hope scores were more strongly associated with higher Existential Well-Being Scores than they were with Religious Well-Being Scores. She judged that the men in her sample had high levels of both spiritual well-being and hope, but that contact with formal religion did not contribute to either. Verna Carson, Karen L. Soeken, Joyce Shanty, and Lillian Terry, "Hope and Spiritual Well-Being: Essentials for Living with AIDS" *Perspectives in Psychiatric Care* 26, 2 (1990): 28–34.

As part of a research project in our department, Bob completed Ellison's Spiritual Well-Being Scale. Bob's scores on the Spiritual Well-Being Scale, very high religious well-being and very low existential well-being, are suggestive of a religious renewal that has not been integrated into the rest of his life. Interestingly, the pattern of his scores differs from the AIDS patients in Carson's study. For her sample the mean scores on both subscales were almost the same, and they were near the midpoint of the scale. In Bob's case his scores on the two subscales were very different, and they were at opposite ends of the scale. Carson's sample was healthier than Bob. They were all outpatients, with an average time since diagnosis of 1.8 years, more than half of Bob's three years.

4. See Westerhoff, *Will Our Children Have Faith?* Using Fowler's model of faith development, I would say that Bob's change represents a step away from the synthetic-conventional stage (3) toward the individuative-reflective stage (4).

5. I have borrowed the term *safe conduct* from psychiatrist Avery D. Weisman, who uses it in a helpful discussion of the physician's role in the care of terminally ill persons with cancer. See his *Coping with Cancer* (New York: McGraw-Hill, 1979), esp. chap. 2.

Chapter 6

GUIDELINES FOR EVALUATING MODELS FOR SPIRITUAL ASSESSMENT

Regardless of the setting in which you work—parish, hospital, counseling center, or something else—you have two choices if you want to use a model for spiritual assessment in your ministry. You can choose a model from those that others have developed, or you can develop one of your own. This chapter is intended to help you make that decision.

In selecting a model to use for spiritual assessment or in developing your own, there are three major issues: (1) your concepts about the spiritual aspect of life; (2) your concepts about norms and authority in the assessment process; and (3) your needs and preferences regarding the spiritual assessment process.[1] In this chapter I will describe each of these three areas. I will use our 7 × 7 model to illustrate how to use these issues as guidelines for evaluating models for spiritual assessment. In the following chapter I will use these guidelines to evaluate three other popular models for spiritual assessment.[2]

Concept of Spirituality

The way in which spirituality or religion is defined is probably the most significant theoretical issue to be considered in evaluating models for spiritual assessment. What is the model's understanding of human nature, its theological anthropology? There are seven issues to be considered as part of this larger question. (1) Is the model's concept of spirituality explicit or implicit? (2) Is it substantive or functional? (3) Does it include one or more dimensions of spiritual life? (4) Is spirituality static or developmental? (5) Is a dynamic perspective included, or are the care recipient's words taken literally? (6) Is the context for spiritual assessment holistic? (7) Is the spiritual dimension distinct from the psychosocial one?

1. Explicit or implicit. In some cases the author's theological beliefs give explicit shape to his or her assessment model. In most of the models with which I am familiar, the theological assumptions that give them shape are implicit.

2. Substantive or functional.   There are two major options for conceptualizing spirituality or religion: focus on *what* a person believes or does, or focus on *how* that person makes meaning in his or her life. The usual approach that many of us take is to focus on what a person believes or does religiously, to use the beliefs of a confessional tradition, either broadly or narrowly, to shape the assessment categories or questions. This is called a substantive definition of spirituality. If a substantive approach is selected, then a caregiver must also decide what beliefs and practices should be included. A rabbi working as a hospital chaplain recently said to me that he thought it was important to ask Jewish patients whether or not they had made a trip to Israel. Whether or not to include such a question is an example of what is involved when using a substantive approach to assessment.

A contrasting approach takes a more functional look at how religious beliefs or practices work in a person's life rather than specifically examining what the beliefs and practices are. James Fowler's work on stages of faith is a well-known example of a primarily functional model. Some models combine both approaches. The model that Fredric Weiss has proposed for spiritual assessment in the inpatient psychiatric context is a good example of one that combines both approaches.[3]

In a setting such as a parish, where we can assume most people will share relatively similar spiritual beliefs and practices, a more substantive model would be appropriate. But a substantive model will probably not be helpful in a more pluralistic setting, such as most hospitals or hospices, where we find great diversity in spiritual beliefs and practices, including people who would not identify themselves as religious or spiritual. In such a setting we run the risk of excluding or distorting the spiritual beliefs and practices of some people because they are not compatible with the categories or questions assumed in our substantive assessment model.

Yet functional approaches also have their problems. Since the functional approach focuses on how people make meaning, any aspect of a person's thought or behavior could be considered here. This approach can thus lead to the conclusion that an avid sports fan's meaning in life comes from the fortunes of his or her favorite athlete. Some will find this is a potentially illuminating possibility. Others will see it as confusing. Another problem is that by focusing primarily on how people find meaning in life, functional models sometimes overlook the rich information contained in the specific substance of their spirituality, in their images of the divine, or in their private meditations, for example. There is no one right approach to this issue. Each caregiver will need to find or develop a model that balances attention to the *what* and the *how* of spiritual life in a manner best suited to his or her specific ministry.

3. More than one dimension.   A third major issue in a model's conceptualization of spirituality is the number of dimensions in the spiritual life that it includes.

The most common approaches to measuring religion are one dimensional; for example, asking people whether or not they believe in God or whether they go to church. Another common one-dimensional approach is to ask people what faith group they identify with: "Are you a Baptist or a Methodist?" The alternative to this is a multidimensional approach that looks at a number of ways religion is manifested in human life. If a model is multidimensional, what dimensions are included? Usually beliefs, practices, experiences, and significant relationships or group activity. Authors such as Clinebell, Fowler, and Ashbrook remind us of the significance of both right- and left-brain functioning. Some caregivers may find it important especially to include right-brain dimensions of spirituality in their assessment.[4]

4. *Static or developmental.*   A fourth issue to consider in the conceptualization of spirituality is whether the model assumes continuity or change in spiritual life. Some models for spiritual assessment, such as Fowler's with his stages of faith, include the idea of spiritual change or development. Other models, McSherry's for example, do not.

5. *Dynamic perspective.*   A fifth issue to consider in the conceptualization of spirituality is whether the model treats religious beliefs and behavior at face value or supports a dynamic exploration of them. That is, we need to know if it enables an assessment of both what people say they believe and feel as well as observations of unconscious attitudes and emotions that might or might not be consistent with those that are consciously held.

6. *Holistic context.*   The sixth question to be considered as part of this issue is what relation between religion and other aspects of human life is assumed or expressed in the model. Is religion treated in isolation from other aspects of life, or are links between religion, culture, personality, family, and health, for example, considered in the model? In most ministry settings a holistic context for spiritual assessment seems to make sense. In some settings it will be essential. This is especially true in cases where the same behavior, or changes in behavior, have different causes. For instance, a preoccupation with a religious idea might be related to an underlying change in the brain's functioning, a reaction to medication, a response to a stressful event, the result of an intrapsychic distress, or a new religious insight.

    We also need to know whether the model makes any assumptions about how the spiritual dimension of life and other dimensions influence one another. If links with other dimensions of human life are considered, what other dimensions are selected, and how are the connections considered? Is spirituality one dimension along with others, as a reading of Pruyser would suggest, or is it the dimension that integrates others?[5] In some models we find that the religious dimension has no real value of its own but is explained in the language or theory of another dimension such as psychology. Draper's famous article, "On the Diagnostic Value of Religious Ideation," illustrates this approach.[6]

7. Distinct from psychosocial aspects.   The seventh question to be considered is a specific example of the issue I have just addressed. What distinction, if any, does the model make between spiritual aspects of life and psychosocial aspects? When Pruyser examined the state of the art in pastoral assessment more than a decade ago, he observed pastors paying little attention to diagnosis. What attention he did observe, he argued, was being focused on psychological assessment.[7] Pruyser deplored this fact and called on pastors to take more seriously their own distinctive perspective on helping others rather than replacing a pastoral assessment with a psychological one.

Yet while calling for a distinct perspective in spiritual assessment, Pruyser failed to recognize the problems that are associated with achieving that perspective. First, it is easiest for religious counselors to achieve a distinct perspective by adopting one variety of substantive approach or another. As I have noted, in pluralistic settings a more functional approach is called for. Second, for those who choose a functional perspective, a major problem, as noted earlier, is difficulty in maintaining a distinction between religious phenomena and all the rest of human behavior. This is one of a number of areas in selecting or developing a model for spiritual assessment in which desired elements seem to be in tension. Each caregiver will have to find the model that is right for his or her context. No one approach will be able to do everything.

Concept of Spirituality in the 7 × 7 Model

I will illustrate the use of these guidelines about the concept of spirituality by using them to evaluate our 7 × 7 model. This model has an implied concept of spirituality. In defining key terms for this book in chapter 1, I explicitly shared my definition of spirituality as the dimension that reflects the need to find meaning in existence and the dimension in which we respond to the sacred. This definition is not an explicit part of the 7 × 7 model, although many will note that it is implicit.

The 7 × 7 model was intentionally developed as a functional approach to spirituality to enable it to be used in pluralistic contexts. Thus the model begins by focusing on how people find meaning in life. But the 7 × 7 model does not stop with a description of how people find meaning. It includes attention to the substantive aspects of a person's spiritual life, including important beliefs, rituals, and relationships. Because the model does not ask any focused, substantive questions, however, it might not uncover important aspects of a person's spiritual background. The caregiver can correct this by including specific substantive questions.

The 7 × 7 model is obviously multidimensional, inquiring about beliefs, religious practices, and key relationships. In the dimension of beliefs and meaning, the model allows for a focus on right-brain aspects of meaning, including images and stories that the person holds to be holy. When we developed the 7 × 7 model, we chose not to include a specific developmental concept of spirituality, such as Fowler's. Yet our dimension of courage and growth acknowledges that for many people the *what* and the *how* of their faith change over time, in both sudden conversions and gradual changes. The 7 × 7 model has a dynamic conception of spirituality. It asks the caregiver to reflect on what the person has said and what the caregiver has observed about the person, and out of that to make interpretations about such things as his or her beliefs and meaning. My observations about the ritual importance for Ethel of the holiday dinners with her family is an example of using the model for a dynamic spiritual assessment.

The 7 × 7 model is the most clearly holistic model for spiritual assessment I am aware of. As is evident in the case examples, this model does not begin the explicit spiritual assessment without first assessing the other dimensions of the person. In part this is a consequence of the model's origin in a health care context where holistic approaches are emphasized. In part it is the result of the way the cases we see in our setting remind us of the important role the other dimensions can play in one's spiritual well-being. But spiritual assessment must be part of holistic assessment in any setting in order to avoid a distorted picture of the person seeking help.

One of the real strengths of the 7 × 7 model is that it distinguishes spiritual assessment from psychosocial assessment, yet it uses a primarily functional approach to spirituality. This is an uncommon combination. The spiritual assessment models that have the greatest distinction between the spiritual and psychosocial dimensions of life usually employ substantive concepts of spirituality. The 7 × 7 model provides a language that can be used to assess the spirituality of a person who does not describe himself or herself as religious. It can be used to describe explicitly the implicit spirituality of the care recipient.

Norms and Authority

The second guideline for evaluating spiritual assessment models addresses the issue of power. Three specific questions related to power should be reviewed. The first question is, What norms for assessment does the model employ, and how explicit are they? The second question is, Does the model assume a context of growth or of dysfunction? The third question is, How is the authority of the respective parties in the assessment process conceptualized in this model? That is, does the patient or parishioner have a passive or active role in focusing the process and defining its results?

In many models for spiritual assessment, the underlying concept of spirituality includes a description about spiritual maturity or health. The question about the norms in a model is thus often directly linked to the question about the model's concept of spirituality. Some models attempt to be more descriptive, to summarize a person's spiritual life in the writer's own terms as much as possible. Other models are more prescriptive, measuring a person's spirituality against the model's standard for spiritual maturity. Models with functional definitions tend to be more descriptive and less normative. Models with more substantive definitions tend to be more prescriptive and normative.

In most models for spiritual assessment the norms that are used to evaluate a person's spiritual maturity are implied. The Religious Status Interview (RSI) developed by Malony illustrates an exception. It has a very explicit definition of "optimal religious functioning," as well as explicit definitions of spiritual maturity for its eight subsections, which are based on Pruyser's framework. According to Malony,

> Mature Christians are those who have identity, integrity, and inspiration. They have "identity" in that their self-understanding is that they are children of God—created by God and destined to live according to a divine plan. They have "integrity" in that their daily life is lived in the awareness that they have been redeemed by God's grace from the guilt of sin and that they can freely respond to God's will in the present. They have "inspiration" in that they live with the sense that God is available to sustain, comfort, encourage, and direct their lives on a daily basis.[8]

Malony's definition shows the way explicit norms for spiritual health or maturity are linked to a substantive concept of spirituality, in Malony's case a Christian concept of spirituality.

The second theme to be considered in evaluating how norms and authority are handled in models for spiritual assessment is whether the model assumes a context of growth or dysfunction. Models that focus on growth are often interested in development, wellness, and prevention. They view problems and crises within that context. Other models of assessment are designed to be used in settings where the focus is on problems, disease, pathology, and restoration.

Whether a model focuses on growth or dysfunction often shapes the specific information that is included for assessment. For example, the diagnostic guidelines of the American Psychiatric Association's DSM-IIIR, are pathology-focused. A complete psychiatric assessment using this model includes something called an Axis IV assessment, an assessment of Severity of Psychosocial Stressors. This assessment reviews the ways in which other problems in an individual's psychosocial world may have contributed to the present mental disorder.[9] A growth-focused model, by contrast, assesses the extent to which an individual's psychosocial world provides key resources that can aid in recovery or help sustain wellness. A model's focus on growth or pathology gives shape to the images, expectations, roles, and thus the behavior of both the person seeking help and the caregiver.

The third theme to be considered is how the authority of the parties in the assessment process is defined, in the process of both information gathering and interpreting or drawing conclusions from the information. We can think of this as a continuum. On one end of the continuum are models that embody the influence of Carl Rogers's client-centered approach to counseling, in which the counselor exercises little diagnostic authority. Pruyser has critically reviewed the influence of this tradition on pastoral care, and Don Browning has described caregivers' related concern to avoid being moralistic.[10] A problem with models on this end of the continuum is that they tend to deny the care recipient the benefit of the caregiver's authority and expertise.

On the other end of the continuum would be models that assume that most of the authority for conducting and interpreting the assessment resides in the caregiver, with the care recipient having a far more passive role. There are problems with these models too. In the brief histories of diagnosis in pastoral care written by both Pruyser and Wayne Oates, stories of authoritarian abuse include the execution of those judged to be possessed by demons; Jonathan Edwards's dictatorial review of one's "signs of gracious affection"; and activist and paternalistic biases of Roman Catholic spiritual direction.[11] In his review, Oates observes a "natural history to the development of diagnostic and statistical manuals" in which they begin as the exciting work of a pioneer who has explored new frontiers in helping others. Gradually such works come to be used in authoritarian ways, with more interest in assigning the correct diagnostic labels than in the person being labeled. Oates writes, "As one studies the classification systems of psychiatric disorders and the classification systems provided by theologians, one sees that this process can be characteristic of both but it certainly need not be so."[12]

Given this history, the question is whether it is possible for caregivers to locate themselves and their power and authority somewhere between the coercive extreme of authoritarian, moralistic pastoral care and the vagueness and indistinct perspective of modern value-neutral pastoral care. Can curious or troubled souls find counselors who will neither burn them at the stake nor leave them at a loss for guidance?

An alternative to both extremes has been described by Pruyser as "a diagnostic partnership."[13] In such a relationship, Pruyser says, "The person is entitled to define for himself [sic], with the help of the expert he seeks out, the nature of his condition, his situation, his self, in the perspective which he finds most relevant."[14] In such a relationship the religious counselor is valuable to a troubled soul not because of his or her lack of authority or perspective, but because he or she makes that perspective available to the person who has come for help. The counselor's knowledge becomes a resource that seekers can employ in their efforts to increase self-understanding and spiritual vitality. The authority of the counselor's perspective is clear and available for another's use. However, any power to coerce another to accept that perspective is eschewed.[15]

There appears to be an inevitable tension between this issue of the authority of the partners in the assessment process and whether or not the model includes a dynamic perspective on spirituality. When we include a dynamic perspective on what people say about their spiritual life, we are by definition introducing a degree of curiosity or suspicion about what they say, and we are assuming the authority to interpret their words or behavior as having a meaning they have not identified and may not agree with. In models of spiritual assessment there is a trade-off between these two factors. Each caregiver will have to find the balance that is best suited to his or her ministry.

Norms and Authority in the 7 × 7 Model

Our aim in developing the 7 × 7 model was that it be used descriptively. Because of the pluralistic context of both patients and chaplains, there were advantages in choosing a model that was descriptive and not normative. We wanted a model that could be used to describe the spirituality of the care recipient with as few assumptions as possible about what spirituality had to include. Although we identified seven spiritual dimensions to be considered in the model, we do not insist that they all be used in every case.

But all models for spiritual assessment have norms. They are either explicit or implicit. Obviously the norms in the 7 × 7 model are implicit. I see four norms in our model. The first can be seen in our belief that there is a spiritual dimension in every person's life, even in those who deny that there is, and in our definition of that dimension as the way they make meaning and relate to the transcendent. The second norm in the 7 × 7 model is expressed in our inclusion of a category for courage and growth. It indicates our assumption that people's spiritual life changes over time, and that more mature spirituality is marked by having the courage to enter into those dark nights of the soul when we give up former beliefs that no longer have meaning, or when we allow the "conversion" of our doubts into a different and more vital spirituality.

The third norm in the 7 × 7 model is expressed in our category of community. We think that healthy spirituality is learned, reinforced, and lived out in relationships with others. We would have to be careful using our model in assessing a hermit. Our category of authority and guidance seems on the surface to be descriptive, but there is a normative aspect in the way it is used in clinical practice. I believe mature spirituality includes some measure of inner authority, so I use this category not only to describe how authority works in a person's life but also to evaluate the strengths and weaknesses of how authority operates in a person's life.

Turning to the second issue related to norms and authority, does the 7 × 7 model focus on growth or dysfunction? I think the model is neutral on this issue. The focus for each of the seven dimensions could be either on the problems a person is having in that area or on that person's resources and strengths. A comprehensive assessment would include attention to both. Thus the 7 × 7 model can be used in contexts such as parishes or retreat centers where the focus is on growth, education, or prevention. It can also be used in health care chaplaincy and counseling centers where a specific problem has precipitated the referral for pastoral care.

Where possible I believe that growth-focused models are the most appropriate ones for spiritual assessment. They reflect the tradition of employing religious or spiritual guidance not only in times of trouble and stress but throughout life. Howard Clinebell has written about this emphasis, saying, "The overarching goal of all pastoral care and counseling (and of all ministry) is to liberate, empower, and nurture wholeness centered in Spirit."[16] Clinebell offers some specific implications of this for pastoral care: "[to] become as aware as possible of the hidden strengths and potential resources of counselees and to affirm these whenever appropriate; . . . to see pathology, brokenness, and sin as truncated, blocked, or distorted growth to a considerable extent; . . . to hold the goal of growth-toward-wholeness in mind throughout the relationship and to articulate this as an expectation and challenge when this is appropriate."[17]

In claiming a preference for this perspective, I am not arguing for a naive view of reality. Rather I am suggesting that an assumption of hope prevail. In this context, as Clinebell writes, the process of growth is accompanied by times of struggle, death, and rebirth, but "the powerful resistances to growth are seen . . . in the context of the more powerful resources for growth."[18]

How does the 7 × 7 model view the respective roles and authority of the caregiver and care recipient? We intentionally developed a tool that would not interfere with the client-centered pastoral practice of allowing people to tell their stories in their own words. Consequently our model was designed not as an interview form but as a framework for organizing and reporting what people communicate about their spirituality in a pastoral conversation.

Because the 7 × 7 model is also a dynamic model, however, tension exists between an open-ended interview in which people can tell their stories in their own words and the interpretation of those stories using the categories of the model. The extent to which the resulting interpretation and care plan are based on the authority of the caregiver or on a diagnostic partnership between the caregiver and care recipient will depend on the caregiver's use of the model in the pastoral relationship.

Pruyser's concept of the diagnostic partnership expresses my preference for the way issues of power and authority should be handled in the process of spiritual assessment. I especially like his description of how the diagnostic "formulation should be arrived at through partnership of the helper and the helped. Ideally it should be so worded that the client or patient can understand it so as to feel free, on the basis of that understanding, to contract for a definable meliorative process."[19] When the goal of spiritual care is wholeness, liberation, and growth, attention must be paid to how the caregiver's authority and power are handled in the process of both counseling and assessment.

Assessment Context and Process

There are five issues to consider in evaluating the context and process of a model for spiritual assessment: 1) the settings in which the model can be used; 2) the form of the model; 3) the relationship of the model to the clinical ministry process; 4) how much training is required to understand the model; and 5) how much time it takes to use the model. As we will see, several of these are related to issues we have discussed in the previous two guidelines.

1. Settings.   One of the first and most practical things we need to know about an assessment model is the context for which it was developed. Is it to be used in parishes, hospices, or psychiatric facilities? Are there any additional contexts in which it can be employed? Some models may have wide applicability across age, gender, or other categories. Other models may be more restricted.

A model such as Malony's, which is based on an explicitly Christian concept of religious maturity, illustrates the way in which the underlying conception of spirituality can affect the contexts in which a given model may be used.[20] Malony's model would obviously not be useful in a pluralistic context in which there were non-Christians. In general, the more diverse the group being served, the more a functional approach to conceptualizing spirituality is necessary.

Most models for spiritual assessment have been developed for use with individuals. A few can be used with small groups.[21] Most models have been designed for use with people who have no cognitive impairment or severe mental illness. Fredric Weiss's model can be used with people with such impairment.[22]

2. Form.   The second issue to consider is the model's form, which may also determine the contexts in which it is useful. Is the model based on a pastoral conversation? Does it require a structured or semistructured interview? Does it include a questionnaire to be completed by the patient or parishioner?

3. *Relation to the clinical ministry process.* The third issue to consider in evaluating the context and process of a model for spiritual assessment is the way the model can be related to the clinical ministry process. By the clinical ministry process I mean the steps of gathering information, interpreting that information, developing goals and a care plan, implementing the plan, evaluating the results of the care provided, and communicating all this to others. I will review each of these steps.

The first step in the clinical ministry process is collecting data. Sometimes this step is referred to as assessment. A model for spiritual assessment needs to be comprehensive. A good model will not leave out information we usually find important to include and will not focus on useless or distracting information. It will highlight important information we might otherwise overlook.

The second step in the clinical ministry process is interpretation of the information that has been gathered in the first step. What does that information add up to? How does the assessment model help us arrive at an answer to that question? Some models list defining characteristics in specific, objective, behavioral terms. If the caregiver sees any behavior from that list, she or he simply assigns the diagnosis indicated.[23] In such models there is almost no need for the caregiver to interpret the significance of the information that was gathered in the first step. Other spiritual assessment models may help the caregiver gather specific information but may offer little assistance in its interpretation.

Related to both information gathering and interpretation is evaluating the level of concreteness or abstraction a model for spiritual assessment employs. Most assessment models use more abstract language. The language used in some models requires special training in order to be used or understood. A model's language may also determine whether it can be adapted for use in research, including research about whether pastoral care caused any change between the time of the first assessment and a later assessment.

A former resident at our center summarized the implications of these first two steps of the clinical ministry process, saying that an ideal model for spiritual assessment would: be complete, all the important phenomena would be attended to; be diverse, different phenomena would have different names; have integrity, the same phenomena would have the same names; be significant, key dimensions of the phenomena would be highlighted; be articulate, relationships among phenomena would be highlighted; be useful, it would facilitate pastoral assessment and development of the pastoral care plan.[24]

The third step in the clinical process is developing the care plan. Does the assessment model result in specific suggestions for pastoral support or intervention? An ideal model for spiritual assessment will be efficient, reducing the trial and error necessary to implement a plan to meet the needs of the person who has come to us for care. As we will see in the next chapter, some models highlight specific problems a person is experiencing and thus facilitate the development of a care plan. Other models are less focused.

The clinical process continues with the pastoral care itself and then begins again with a new assessment to review what changes may have occurred as a result. In evaluating a model for spiritual assessment, caregivers should notice whether it assumes one assessment is sufficient or whether it suggests reassessment at intervals that make sense in their settings.

We also want to look at how the model helps us communicate each of these steps to others who should know or might be interested in them. This brings us back to the issue of the language the models use, both for information gathering and for interpreting and summarizing the spiritual assessment. Is it language that those who are not professional caregivers would understand? If so, the model would meet Pruyser's norm that the care recipient be a partner in performing the assessment and drawing conclusions from it. We should also note whether it is language that colleagues from other professional disciplines would understand, thus giving them a sense of how the spiritual aspect of this person's situation is related to the rest of his or her life.

4. Training. The fourth aspect of this guideline is closely linked to what I have just described. How much theological or psychological training is required to understand and use the model? Does it summarize its conclusions in a manner that parishioners or counselees will be able to understand for themselves, or in a way that professionals from other disciplines will be able to understand? Some models, such as Fowler's, contain many technical concepts, and extensive training is required to use or understand these assessments. Many hospice spiritual assessment models, by contrast, were developed so that nurses or social workers would be able to conduct an initial spiritual assessment and know which cases indicated a need for referral to the chaplain.

5. Time. The final issue to consider is how much time it takes to use the model. This includes the time to gather the initial information, the time to interpret that information, to document the assessment in whatever manner is appropriate to the setting, and the time to communicate the assessment and care plan to other significant persons.

The time required is frequently related to the model's form. Models with questionnaires, checklists, or those based on specific behavioral signs usually require the least time. Models with semistructured and open-ended interviews probably take the most time. Naturally the most comprehensive models take the most time. Models that make fewer demands on time are usually less comprehensive.

Assessment Context and Process in the 7 × 7 Model

Although we developed the 7 × 7 model for use in an acute health care setting, one of its strengths is that it can be used almost anywhere, including parishes, counseling centers, and hospices. It was also intended to be used with people from different faiths. I have seen it used only with individuals, but it could be used in small groups. The 7 × 7 model could also be used to summarize the information gathered in a spiritual assessment of a child or a person with cognitive impairments. Although the language of the model is broad, several efforts have been made to modify the categories for research and clinical use.[25]

A strength of the model for the information-gathering aspect of the clinical ministry process is its comprehensiveness. It directs our attention to important information and frequently reminds us of some areas we might have neglected but would subsequently have found quite helpful in understanding the case. The biggest problem I have found with the model in the health care context is that it does not specifically include attention to actual or potential ethical dilemmas, such as withdrawing life-sustaining treatment, if the patient or family does not mention them.

Like most spiritual assessment models, the 7 × 7 model does not provide specific assistance in the process of interpreting information that has been gathered about a person's spiritual life. It does set the stage for deciding what might be included in a pastoral care plan.

The categories in the 7 × 7 model are not difficult to understand, and caregivers can begin to apply them to their cases in the first encounter. The category that causes the most confusion is courage and growth. Many people assume it means a stoic or brave response to suffering. Rather we intended courage to describe the willingness to let go of cherished beliefs, revise them, or take hold of new beliefs. The model does not require extensive specialized training, but the more training caregivers have, the more sophisticated their use of the model can be in information gathering, interpreting, and in planning for pastoral care.

The simplicity of the terms in the model makes it easy for a caregiver to communicate reports of assessments to care recipients and to colleagues from other disciplines, especially if the language and concepts one uses to elaborate on the seven dimensions is not too technical.

The 7 × 7 model requires a considerable amount of time, especially in a hospital setting. A full assessment of all the dimensions can take more time than most chaplains in acute care settings can afford. The model is flexible, however, and can be modified for more elaborate or more simplified reports.

It can also be used in several stages, with a simplified, tentative, initial assessment, and later a more comprehensive follow-up assessment.

NOTES

1. There is some similarity between this framework and the one Don Browning describes for practical moral reasoning. Defining the concept of spirituality is related to Browning's metaphorical level, defining norms and issues of authority to the obligational level, and defining the assessment process to the level of rules and roles. See Browning, *Religious Ethics and Pastoral Care*, 53ff.

There are also parallels between these three issues and Steven Ivy's discussion of the *what* (concept of spirituality) and the *how* (assessment process) of spiritual assessment. See Steven S. Ivy, "Pastoral Assessment: Issues and Directions," *Religious Studies Review* 16, 3 (July 1990): 212–18; and idem, "The Structural-Developmental Theories of James Fowler and Robert Kegan as Resources for Pastoral Assessment" (Ph.D. diss. Southern Baptist Theological Seminary, Louisville, Ky., 1985), esp. 16ff.

2. Three other discussions of criteria or guidelines for evaluating models for spiritual assessment can be found in Pruyser, *The Minister as Diagnostician*, 61; Carl D. Schneider, "Faith Development and Pastoral Diagnosis," in *Faith Development and Fowler*, ed. Craig Dykstra and Sharon Parks (Birmingham, Ala.: Religious Education Press, 1986), 221–50; and Ivy, "Theories." For a discussion focusing on nursing models of spirituality and spiritual care, see Janet Mayer, "Wholly Responsible for a Part, or Partly Responsible for a Whole: The Concept of Spiritual Care in Nursing," *Second Opinion* 17, 3 (January 1992): 26–55.

3. Fowler, *Stages of Faith;* Weiss, "Pastoral Care Planning."

4. See Fowler, *Stages of Faith*, 24, 104; Clinebell, *Basic Types*, 36. See also James B. Ashbrook, *The Human Mind and the Mind of God: Theological Promise in Brain Research* (Lanham, Md.: University Press of America, 1985).

5. These two options are helpfully diagramed in Farran, "Development of a Model for Spiritual Assessment and Intervention," *Journal of Religion and Health* 28, 3 (Fall 1989): 185–94.

6. Edgar Draper, George G. Meyer, Zane Parzen, and Gene Samuelson, "On the Diagnostic Value of Religious Ideation," *Archives of General Psychiatry* 13 (September 1965): 202–7.

7. Pruyser, *The Minister as Diagnostician*, 39, 27.

8. Malony, "Clinical Assessment," 6–7.

9. APA, *DSM-IIIR*, 18–20.

10. Pruyser, *The Minister as Diagnostician*, 39ff., Browning, *Religious Ethics*, chap. 3.

11. Pruyser, *The Minister as Diagnostician*, 30ff. Also see Wayne Oates, *The Religious Care of the Psychiatric Patient* (Philadelphia: Westminster Press, 1978), 87–95.

12. Oates, *Religious Care*, 93.

13. Pruyser, *The Minister as Diagnostician*, 80ff.

14. Ibid., 83.

15. For a similar perspective, see Browning, *Religious Ethics*, 102.

16. Clinebell, *Basic Types*, 26.

17. Ibid., 89, 91.

18. Ibid., 60.

19. Pruyser, *The Minister as Diagnostician*, 83.

20. Malony, "Clinical Assessment."

21. See Glen Sackett, "Seven Dimensions of Spirituality," *Care Giver* 1, 2 (November 1985): 27–30.

22. Weiss, "Pastoral Care Planning."

23. For an example, see Milton W. Hay, "Principles in Building Spiritual Assessment Tools," *American Journal of Hospice Care*, September/October 1989, 25–31.

24. My thanks to John Weston for this summary.

25. My colleague Don Camp at the Children's Memorial Hospital in Chicago has done some work on a version that might be used in a pediatric setting. Our original research team generated a list of behavioral-specific questions for each of the seven dimensions. More recently I have identified specific descriptors from other research and writing that could be used for each dimension.

Chapter 7

REVIEW OF THREE MODELS FOR SPIRITUAL ASSESSMENT

To put the guidelines presented in the previous chapter into practice, I will now evaluate three models of spiritual assessment: Paul Pruyser's, Elisabeth McSherry's, and the diagnostic category "spiritual distress" of the North American Nursing Diagnosis Association. I chose these three models for several reasons. They include some of the most widely known and influential works on spiritual assessment. They represent an interesting variety of approaches to spiritual assessment. They can be and have been used in a variety of ministry settings. All of them are available in publications for those who wish to study them further.[1]

Paul Pruyser

Paul Pruyser's 1976 book, *The Minister as Diagnostician,* is one of the most influential works on spiritual assessment. Ironically Pruyser was not a pastor; he was a psychologist. However, he had a strong interest in pastoral care and counseling. He was frequently a consultant to pastoral care and counseling training programs, professional organizations, and theological schools. Many people in pastoral care knew him as a friend and colleague and respected him as a scholar and writer.

Pruyser's aim in writing *Minister as Diagnostician* was not to teach pastors how to do spiritual assessment but rather to encourage pastors to be more deliberate about including spiritual assessment as a part of their work. Although Pruyser did not intend for his book to become a manual for spiritual assessment, the seven themes he identifies in his fifth chapter have become the foundation of more specific models of spiritual assessment than perhaps any other source.[2]

Pruyser frames his work as an effort to change pastors' self-deprecating description of themselves as jacks-of-all-trades and masters of none.[3] In Pruyser's view, each professional discipline has a distinct perspective on the human condition. No one profession can claim to have the only real or true perspective. Rather each profession has a partial view. The greater the number of different perspectives we can bring to a person's problems, the more likely we are to generate an adequate understanding of that person.

In the period after the Second World War, Pruyser observed that pastors had no diagnostic framework of their own to contribute to the multidisciplinary dialogue occurring in health care. Rather they seemed to be strongly attracted to the language of psychological diagnosis. When he talked with pastors, he reported, they said that "their basic theological disciplines were of little help to them in ordering their observations and planning their meliorative moves."[4] Pruyser was distressed by this. He thought pastors ought to claim their distinct diagnostic perspective. In order to assist this process, he briefly reviewed the ways pastoral diagnosis was performed in earlier periods in the church. However, when he concluded this review, he criticized the authoritarian and legalistic approach to pastoral diagnosis that it revealed. Turning to the modern period, Pruyser reviewed the influence on pastors of Carl Rogers's client-centered type of therapy. He saw Rogers's work as having contributed to pastors' lack of interest in pastoral diagnosis.

Pruyser believed that when people turned to pastors they wanted to review their problems in the light of a theological perspective. However, he acknowledged that pastors "have a hard time finding appropriate theological categories for approaching their patients and responding to their needs."[5] To help with this problem Pruyser offered some "Guidelines for Pastoral Diagnosis" in chapter 5 of his book. The guidelines are in the form of seven theological themes. Pruyser suggested that as pastors listen to their parishioners, they listen for the ways the story the person shares is related to the themes. I will list Pruyser's seven themes and key questions that elaborate each theme for the most part taken from his text.

PRUYSER'S GUIDELINES FOR PASTORAL DIAGNOSIS

1. Awareness of the Holy
   - what, if anything, is sacred, revered
   - any experiences of awe or bliss, when, in what situations
   - any sense of mystery, of anything transcendent
   - any sense of creatureliness, humility, awareness of own limitations
   - any idolatry, reverence displaced to improper symbols

2. Providence
   - what is God's intention toward me
   - what has God promised me
   - belief in cosmic benevolence
   - related to capacity for trust
   - extent of hoping versus wishing

3. Faith
   - affirming versus negating stance in life

- able to commit self, to engage
- open to world or constricted

4. Grace or Gratefulness
   - kindness, generosity, the beauty of giving and receiving
   - no felt need for grace or gratefulness
   - forced gratitude under any circumstances
   - desire for versus resistance to blessing

5. Repentance
   - the process of change from crookedness to rectitude
   - a sense of agency in one's own problems or one's response to them versus being a victim versus being too sorry for debatable sins
   - feelings of contrition, remorse, regret
   - willingness to do penance

6. Communion
   - feelings of kinship with the whole chain of being
   - feeling embedded or estranged, united or separated in the world, in relations with one's faith group, one's church

7. Sense of Vocation
   - willingness to be a cheerful participant in creation
   - signs of zest, vigor, liveliness, dedication
   - aligned with divine benevolence or malevolence
   - humorous and inventive involvement in life versus grim and dogmatic

Following his description of these themes, Pruyser discussed the relationship between the parties in the pastoral diagnostic process. He described this relationship as a diagnostic partnership. For Pruyser, pastoral diagnosis did not mean labeling people. It meant assisting them in their process of spiritual self-assessment. In the pastoral diagnostic process, Pruyser wrote, "The person is entitled to define for himself [sic], with the help of the expert he seeks out, the nature of his condition, his situation, his self, in the perspective which he finds most relevant."[6] In the rest of the book Pruyser discussed the role of religious language in pastoral diagnosis and options for ways a pastor and psychiatrist can work together in providing care rather than one professional always referring the case to the other. In his final chapter Pruyser included five case vignettes to illustrate the process of pastoral diagnosis.

Evaluating Paul Pruyser's Model for Spiritual Assessment

This evaluation of the strengths and weaknesses of Pruyser's discussion of pastoral diagnosis uses the three guidelines—concept of spirituality, approach to norms and authority, and assessment context and process—described in the previous chapter.

Concept of Spirituality. What is a pastoral diagnosis for Pruyser? His work offers no explicit answer to that question. Pruyser's stance is that pastoral diagnoses are assessments made from the pastoral perspective by pastors. This response assumes a widespread agreement about what is involved in the pastoral perspective. The popularity of Pruyser's seven themes could be seen as evidence that such widespread, implicit agreement about the pastoral perspective does exist.

Pruyser's model of pastoral diagnosis is a creative blend of both functional and substantive approaches to spirituality. He was interested both in how people find meaning and in what that meaning is. His interest in how people find meaning is reflected, for example, in his discussion of his seven guidelines. "I see them . . . as multidimensional themes which, in the mind of the pastoral interviewer, provide vistas of the person's organization of meanings, at multiple levels and with greater or lesser cohesiveness."[7] This interest in how people make meaning also runs throughout his description of the seven guidelines for pastoral diagnosis. For example, in discussing a person's attitude toward the Bible, he said, "The diagnostic value of that symbol of faith lies in what it does to the person's horizon. Does it open up the world for him, or does it draw narrow boundaries, making a little niche for an area of safety?"[8]

Although Pruyser used his seven guidelines in a functional way, the seven themes in the guidelines reflect his Reformed Protestant heritage. In that sense his conception of spirituality is also substantive. To the extent that a person does not share the substance of Pruyser's faith, these guidelines might contribute to a misassessment, either because important themes were overlooked or because the wrong themes were emphasized. For example, Pruyser's guidelines make no mention of Jesus Christ. They permit, and indeed encourage, open-ended conversation and inquiry. But the absence of Christ would be a serious omission for a person from an evangelical Protestant tradition. More obviously, Pruyser's themes would not be the best choice for spiritual assessment of devout Jews or Buddhists, for example. Still, the seven themes that constitute the substance of Pruyser's approach to pastoral diagnosis are important themes in many faiths. The breadth of their relevance combined with Pruyser's application of them to understand both the *what* and the *how* of a person's spirituality has contributed to the strength of this model for spiritual assessment and its widespread adoption.

Pruyser's approach to pastoral diagnosis also takes into account several key dimensions of spirituality. In his discussion of his guidelines he referred to an interest in beliefs and in the impact beliefs have on the duties and obligations a person feels. He was also interested in a person's relationships, both in the relationships that help form and sustain faith and in the impact of the person's beliefs on his or her relationships with others. In his guidelines Pruyser also referred to rituals and devotional practices.

Pruyser's description of religious life does not refer to an explicit framework of spiritual or faith development, such as we find in the work of Fowler or Westerhoff.[9] But in his discussion of religious life he was aware that important changes take place in the life of faith, between guilt and forgiveness or enthusiasm and caution, for example.

Pruyser's approach to pastoral diagnosis is a good example of a model that employs a dynamic perspective on spirituality; that is, Pruyser encouraged an approach to assessment that does not assume that what people literally say is all we can know about them. He suggested a hermeneutic of suspicion. "As diagnosticians, pastors should be immediately curious about the gods of their clients, not taking their God-talk for granted but trying to find out what it refers to in thought and action."[10] It is uncommon to find models of spiritual assessment that combine a dynamic perspective of spirituality with a substantive conception of spirituality. Pruyser's model combines these two approaches constructively.

In his discussion of pastoral diagnosis Pruyser took a holistic approach. As I mentioned earlier, one of the concerns that led Pruyser to write this book was his observation that the pastoral or theological perspective was not being represented in interdisciplinary care settings. "Pain and suffering are always complex and multidimensional experiences often crying out for enlightenment and resolution in several perspectives at once."[11] Pruyser obviously preferred that pastoral assessment take place in and contribute to a multidisciplinary assessment.

The final component to review in Pruyser's concept of spirituality is the way he defined the relation between the spiritual aspect and the psychosocial aspect of life. While calling for pastors to recover the contributions of their distinct pastoral perspective, at a number of points Pruyser himself relied on psychoanalytic concepts in order to describe some elements of the theological themes he suggested as guidelines for pastoral diagnosis.[12] How can we account for Pruyser's use of the perspective of psychology to elaborate on aspects of the themes he recommended for the pastoral perspective? I would see it as a reflection of the complexity of this task, a complexity that Pruyser seems to minimize in this text.[13]

Pruyser described the post-World War II pastor's interest in psychological assessment as simply a "suspicion of the relevance of theology."[14] In contrast, I see it as a constructive effort to respond to three trends. The first was the awareness that traditional models for spiritual assessment were employed in an authoritarian and legalistic fashion and had little to offer regarding discerning a person's specific spiritual needs. As I have noted, Pruyser was well aware of this pattern. The second trend was this period's radical questioning of all traditional authority, including religious authority. This perspective was most dramatically exemplified in the "death of God" theologies. We see it continuing in the efforts of some scholars to construct postmodern theologies. The third trend, occurring at the same time, was the discovery of the rich resources modern psychology was offering for understanding and responding to human pain and suffering.

Pruyser seems aware of the second trend, having mentioned the ways in which theological language was subject to a variety of theoretical critiques "and a host of other denigrating epithets current in the ambiance of Oxford and Cambridge."[15] He went on to say he did "not deny the validity of such critical arguments," but he did question their "potency."[16] By that he meant that the critical arguments had no impact on the significance of traditional religious language for ordinary believers.

Pruyser's analysis fails to take into account the impact of these movements on the pastors of the period. Fowler's theory of stages of faith development might be helpful in understanding what was going on here. Using Fowler's perspective, we could say that the tools of higher biblical criticism, psychoanalytic theories about the origins of religious faith, and other developments in philosophy and science during the first half of the twentieth century led many pastors, especially those with an interest in the specialty of pastoral care and counseling, away from a conventional faith perspective (Fowler's stage 3) in which the symbolic nature of the language of faith was basically unquestioned. These pastors moved to a more reflective perspective on faith (Fowler's stage 4), where the logical consistency of religious language and its ability to respond to critical challenges from culture were more significant. Pruyser's challenge to pastors to renew their interest in traditional religious language and symbols comes more as an urge to regress to the conventional stage of faith development. An alternative would have been a model that showed how both the symbolic truth of traditional religious language and the truth of philosophical and scientific critiques of religious language could be held together in a conjunctive style of faith (Fowler's stage 5).[17]

Although I disagree with Pruyser's analysis of how pastors came to lose their distinct perspective in human need, his work has played a significant role in calling this issue to our attention. The concept of spirituality embodied in his mixed functional and substantive approach to his seven guidelines has offered caregivers, whose own way of making meaning might be characterized by Fowler's stages 3, 4, or 5, a model of how to do distinctly pastoral diagnosis without losing the important advances provided by dynamic psychology.

Norms and Authority. What did Pruyser say about norms and authority in the process of pastoral diagnosis? Pruyser was not explicit about the norms on which he based his model. He assumed he was addressing an audience who shared his view of the content of the pastoral perspective, which is based on the normative beliefs of Reformed Protestant Christianity. Insofar as a person's spirituality differs from those beliefs, Pruyser's model, and those based on it, run the risk of distorting the assessment of that person's spiritual life.

Pruyser's book assumes a context in which a person has come to a pastor seeking help with a problem. However, nothing in the content of his model limits it to use in situations of crisis, distress, or problem solving. It could be a very useful tool to guide spiritual assessment for individuals or groups in a congregational context who want to review and strengthen their spiritual lives.

Pruyser's description of the role of the parties in the assessment process, the diagnostic partnership, strikes a delicate balance between nondirective and authoritarian approaches to care. Pruyser felt that parishioners came to their pastoral caregivers expecting them to respond from a distinctly pastoral perspective. Yet, as Pruyser described it, that response seeks to join with parishioners in their own growing spiritual self-understanding.[18]

Pruyser encouraged a hermeneutic of suspicion in which parishioners' literal reports of their beliefs or religious practices might be viewed in the larger perspective of what their behavior and emotions also indicate about their spiritual lives. He carried this into his description of the relationship between parishioner and caregiver, recognizing the possibility that parishioners' expectations of the pastor may not be completely rational, but rather may be distorted by the transference of feelings from other earlier relationships onto the relationship with the pastor.[19] When a model for spiritual assessment includes this dynamic perspective, it is usually at the cost of any recognition of the authority of the person being assessed. Pruyser's commitment to respect for the authority of the person being assessed and the dynamic perspective is a powerful but rare combination. It requires a mature caregiver to be able to hold these principles together in actual practice.

Assessment Context and Process.   In what kinds of ministry settings can Pruyser's model be used? It is applicable in a wide range of ministry settings. The cases in his book illustrate its use in both parishes and psychiatric hospitals. As the references in the notes to this chapter show, it has also been adapted for use in general hospitals, in chemical dependency recovery programs, and in correctional settings.

What is the form of Pruyser's model, and what are the implications of its form for its use? Pruyser suggested that the guidelines be used to inform a caregiver's reflections on an unfolding pastoral conversation. Referring to his seven categories, he wrote, "The words I proposed should *linger in the pastor's mind, functioning as guideposts to his* [sic] *diagnostic thinking.*"[20] The emphasis he gave these words suggest Pruyser's strong feelings about this matter. Elsewhere he wrote that using the categories to develop a structured interview would be "a gross distortion of my intention."[21] Pruyser's seven categories have been adapted into structured interviews and questionnaires in published and unpublished spiritual assessment models, so it appears that the model can be adapted for use in a variety of forms.

Pruyser's model for spiritual assessment is most helpful with the information-gathering portion of the pastoral care process. It directs attention to a number of significant aspects of spiritual life, at least several of which are likely to be salient for any given person. The model, like most, offers no guidance on how the information obtained should be interpreted or its implications for a pastoral care plan. These aspects of the pastoral care process are left to the caregiver's judgment.

Considerable training is probably required to be able to use Pruyser's model in pastoral care. Several factors contribute to this. First, the model contains terms with theological connotations such as providence, communion, and vocation. Without some training a caregiver might easily think that communion referred to a sacrament. In fact it refers to a person's sense of membership in the world and participation with others. This points to the fact that people in other professional disciplines would also need some training in order to be able to understand and benefit from a Pruyser-based pastoral assessment as a part of a holistic care plan.

The model is designed for use in open-ended pastoral conversations, and it encourages insight into the reality behind a person's verbal self-descriptions. Training is required to learn how to conduct such an interview effectively. Even more training is necessary in order to be able to apply a psychodynamic interpretative framework in an accurate and helpful way. Perhaps most demanding is, as I have already mentioned, cultivating the ability to respect both the parishioner's perspective on his or her spiritual life and one's own use of a dynamic interpretative perspective.

Developing a spiritual assessment based on Pruyser's model would be moderately time consuming. It would take time to conduct the pastoral conversation and then additional time to write a summary of the assessment. The amount of time each of these activities took could vary in practice, depending on the needs and specifics of a given case. It would also be possible to use the model to summarize an assessment that was developed in several stages; a brief initial interview and assessment and a more extensive set of conversations and spiritual assessment report when called for.

In summary, Pruyser's pioneering work on pastoral diagnosis left us with a set of theological categories that have been widely adapted for spiritual assessment in a variety of ministry contexts. The model's conception of spirituality is sophisticated and complex. For the most part it makes possible a distinctly spiritual assessment, but one that is dynamically informed. Pruyser's work is a model for balancing the autonomy of the person being assessed with a dynamic approach to assessment. For some, the drawbacks of Pruyser's model are the training and time required to use it.

Elisabeth McSherry

Elisabeth McSherry, a physician who works at the Brockton/West Roxbury Veterans Administration Medical Center in Massachusetts, has been helping pastoral caregivers develop their "clinical science." By clinical science she means "a specialized body of knowledge, a clinical science practice method, common conventions, specialties and research."[22] She believes that if chaplains adopt this approach, they will have an objective basis on which to improve their patient care and accountability. The goals of this approach are also to enable chaplains to make better care plans for individual patients and to document any changes that are the result of pastoral care. It helps chaplains to assess the spiritual needs and resources of groups of patients with common diagnoses as well. This approach is also intended to help chaplains demonstrate the contributions of pastoral care to reducing the overall costs of hospital care.[23]

According to McSherry, a key element in developing the clinical science of chaplaincy and achieving these goals is the pastoral caregiver's assessment of the patient's spiritual needs. Her model for spiritual assessment has two major components: the Spiritual Profile Assessment (SPA) and the Semi-Structured Interview (SSI). The data from these two tools can be compiled on a one-page form, the Computer Data Information Sheet. There is also a Clinical Assessment Data Card, which is used to record initial assessment information, follow-up care, and changes in areas of interest.[24]

The SPA is a set of three questionnaires that most patients can complete themselves. The first instrument is the Personal Health Inventory. This is a modification, developed by Granger Westberg, of the well-known Holmes/Rahe Stress Scale.[25] In addition to the original stress scale items, it includes six items about the spiritual dimension of the person's life and five questions about current concerns and goals. The second item in the SPA is a Religiosity Index. It is based on research by Zuckerman, Kasl, and Ostfeld.[26] It is a three-question measure of attendance at religious services and the importance of religious beliefs. The third item is called the Ultimate Values Test. It asks respondents to indicate the three most important values in their life by selecting from a list of eighteen values. The tool is based on the work of Rokeach and McCready and Greeley.[27] Examples of values on the list include knowing and loving God, family security, and good health. McSherry provides instructions for scoring the three items in the SPA. How these scores can be used clinically is not described beyond suggesting that the findings be discussed with patients to help them clarify their values as well as identify stresses or other changes they wish help with.

The SSI, Semi-Structured Interview, is a series of questions that a chaplain can use to guide an initial interview with a patient. It is described as a resource both for spiritual assessment and for developing "an automated database that helps departments discover major trends and needs in various groups of patients"[28] It offers the chaplain a way to begin to talk with a patient about explicitly religious concerns. McSherry says it is designed to help chaplains overcome their "personal discomfort in talking about their relationship with God."[29] The interview begins with an inquiry about the patient's church attendance and feelings toward their pastor. Once started, the expectation is that the pastoral interview will proceed with ease.

In addition to background and demographic information, the SSI contains four major areas. The first area is the significant others of the patient, including their names and relationships to the patient. The second area, relationship quality, includes information about the patient's image of God, relationship with God, relationship with chaplain and/or pastor, and practice of attendance at worship, if any. The specific questions and response options in this area are

1. *Does the person go to church? Why? Why not?*
   (attendance at religious services)
   A. attends; note frequency, e.g., "weekly"
   B. via media
   C. nonattendance, reasons:
      1) not interested
      2) difficult access
      3) angry
      4) other
2. *How does the person relate to his or her clergy? Why? Why not?*
3. *How religious/nonreligious does the person see him- or herself?*
   5   very religious
   4   fairly religious
   3   only slightly religious
   2   not at all religious
   1   against religion
4. *How does the person think of God? (relationship quality)*
   A. Style of relationship with God (enter code letter)
      P   personal
      I   impersonal
      T   transiently remote (e.g., "Once in a while I pray to God")
   B. Image of God (enter code letter)
      E   early: like own parents
      M   mature: biblically balanced
      U   unformed/undeveloped

The third area, called spiritual resources, is a checklist of the following spiritual resources:

faith
hope
meaning/purpose
self-esteem
personalized prayer (prayer for oneself and others)
scriptural resource (biblical literacy and understanding used with prayer)
faith community (church/parish life in which the patient/client actively
    participates and enjoys)
coherent theistic belief system (grade 1–5)
    1. personal (intercessory only)
    2. broader interaction with God (praise, thanks, intercessory for
       others, guidance, meditation)
    3. active personal ministry (assumes prayer as in 2, with active
       outputs by individual)
    4. never developed
    5. stagnant

The fourth area is a list of ten spiritual concerns commonly found among hospitalized persons. In the original SSI the presence or absence of the concern is indicated. The Salisbury article indicates that the level of concern is rated on a scale from 1 to 10. The ten concerns are:

anger toward God
anticipatory grief
concern about afterlife
dying transition
grief
inner conflict about beliefs
moral and ethical nature of medical plan
shame
suffering/theodicy
unrelieved guilt

The information from the SPA and the SSI is recorded on the Computer Data Information Sheet. This allows for efficient pastoral care record keeping as well as research. There is additional space on the sheet to record sacramental information, such as the most recent dates for the sacrament of the sick and communion, the quality of the relationship with chaplain, and the name of the patient's local pastor.

McSherry and her colleagues have published a number of papers related to their model of assessment. The most extensive case report using the model, the case of Mr. M., a fifty-two-year-old white male with a spinal cord injury, is contained in the article by Salisbury, et al.[30]

Evaluation of McSherry's
Model for Spiritual Assessment

Concept of Spirituality. In her model, McSherry offers no explicit discussion of the concept of spirituality or the theological beliefs that helped shape her model.

Initially the model appears to take a broad approach to conceptualizing spirituality. On closer examination of the choices for several items, it is evident that the model was developed with the beliefs and practices of traditional, evangelical Protestantism in mind. This is seen in categories for image of God, relationship with God, and coherent belief system. It is perhaps most explicit in the preface to the SSI, where McSherry says, "People today are hungering for the spiritual. They are thirsty for God. . . .They are seeking to have a personal relationship with Him."[31]

McSherry basically employs a substantive approach to conceptualizing spirituality. Her SPA and SSI focus specifically on what people believe, what their prayers are like, and what their spiritual concerns are. Her writings do not give an indication of an awareness of a functional approach to spiritual assessment or of the pros or cons of one approach or the other.

The concept of spirituality in her model is multidimensional, including religious beliefs, practices, needs, and significant relationships. The modified Personal Health Inventory contains two questions about changes in relationship with God and in church activity or prayer. These are the major referents to changes in the model's concept of spirituality. The model does not appear to employ a concept of growth or development as part of its concept of spirituality. The model also has no hermeneutic of suspicion in its perspective on spirituality. The statements and actions of a patient appear to be taken literally, at face value.

A strong holistic interest is built into this model. McSherry is interested in studies of how religion affects healing and health, and thus the assessment includes data from other dimensions of human life, most notably in its Personal Health Inventory. Unfortunately the model has no explicit place to note concurrent psychological problems, such as depression or personality disorders, which even in nonpsychiatric hospitals appear to be common complications in cases to which chaplains are referred. While the concept of spirituality in this model is holistic, the model maintains a clear and distinct focus on the religious aspects of the patient's life primarily by employing a focused substantive concept of spirituality.

Norms and Authority. The norms in the model are implicit. McSherry does not claim to be developing a model of spiritual assessment for evangelical Protestants. Yet the concept of spirituality implied in her interview indicates that this is the framework she has adopted. To the extent that a patient does not share this belief system, this model might not provide the best summary of his or her spiritual strengths and needs.

McSherry's model was developed for use in the hospital context, and thus an assumption of spiritual need or distress is appropriately part of her model. She has balanced this, however, by including a section assessing the spiritual resources available to the patient. Many models of spiritual assessment designed for health care contexts focus only on the patient's or family's spiritual problems or needs. McSherry's inclusion of the patient's spiritual resources is one of the strengths of her model.

McSherry does not explicitly discuss the respective roles and authority of those involved in the assessment process. However, the assessment is obviously interested in eliciting the patient's statement of his or her concerns and values and focusing pastoral support and intervention in the service of the patient's articulated aims. Items in the Personal Health Inventory about the patient's goals and the use of the Ultimate Values Inventory, as well as the section on spiritual concerns in the SSI, facilitate this patient-centered focus. The Salisbury case gives a good example of how pastoral care can be implemented based on the information about the patient's goals and values obtained with these tools.

Assessment Context and Process. McSherry's model has a number of features that link it specifically to ministry in the health context, including the use of the stress scale and the specific spiritual concerns listed in the SSI. It assumes that the pastoral caregiver and patient are strangers to each other. It directs attention to information that both chaplains and other health professionals would find useful in getting acquainted with a new patient, for example, family support and ultimate values. The model is also recommended for use in community health screening, and it is easy to see its value in such a setting. This tool would be useful in a parish setting, especially for parish nurses but also for pastors. It also seems useful for nursing homes and other long-term care settings. It does not have any items about the spiritual needs of family members or significant others, suggesting its origins in a setting where family may not usually be included as unit of care. As I have already mentioned, this assessment seems best suited for a population that shares McSherry's evangelical Protestant approach to spirituality.

The two methods in the model, the questionnaires of the SPA and the Semi-Structured Interview, may cause problems for some pastoral caregivers or patients. These are quite different from the less structured pastoral conversation that usually characterizes information gathering in pastoral care.

Many caregivers might reject these methods as inappropriately impersonal for their work. I hope that caregivers give them a try first. Both methods can be used in ways that communicate personal concern and caring. Of course they can also be used in very impersonal ways. Their advantage is that they enable the caregiver to obtain a lot of information about the patient's background and current situation in a relatively short time. As time becomes a more precious commodity in health care ministry, methods such as this may help us to be more focused and thus more effective.

As a tool to aid pastoral caregivers with the clinical ministry process, McSherry's model has its strengths and weaknesses. A key strength is the concreteness and specificity of the information it obtains. The items in the list of spiritual concerns and elsewhere in the model appear to have been selected by someone who knew what chaplains most needed to know when they meet a new patient. The model's strength is its clear and direct focus on the practically important information about the religious beliefs, practices, and needs of hospital patients.

Another strength is the way the model focuses attention on information, such as the patient's spiritual concerns, that is not just interesting but that has important implications for developing the pastoral care plan. Using McSherry's model, it is relatively easy to generate care plans that address the spiritual concerns identified by the patient and that employ the spiritual resources and ultimate values the patient has identified as important. The Salisbury case is a good illustration of this process. Although the approach to ministry in that case was more directive than eductive, the work focused on the concerns the patient identified in the assessment process. Very little interpretation about the central concerns of the patient was necessary in moving from assessment to intervention.

Another strength of the model in terms of data gathering is the Personal Health Inventory. This tool focuses attention on major changes in the patient's life in the past twelve months. In pastoral assessment we sometimes look only at a problem's immediate context, neglecting the larger context, which may be a factor in the current problem. The Health Inventory invites the patient to think about the larger context of his or her life and any important changes that have taken place. This not only may shed light on factors contributing to the current problem but also provides an opportunity to discuss with patients how they experienced these changes and what they meant for them over time.

A weakness of McSherry's model for data gathering is related to one of its strengths. Certain categories in the SSI, for example, the difference between the types of relationship to God (person-to-person, distant or passing relationship), offer no clear criteria by which to determine the category a patient should be placed in. Another weakness related to the specificity of the model is the apparent lack of flexibility in the categories. What if a patient has a spiritual concern that is not part of the list, or uses different language when referring to spiritual matters? In conducting an assessment interview it would be important for a caregiver to be alert to possible spiritual needs that are not in this inventory, perhaps by initially asking a more open-ended question before reviewing the list with a patient. The options listed for spiritual concerns are simple and specific, but they may not allow the flexibility needed to account for the uniqueness, the individuality, of human suffering as we encounter it in many pastoral care settings.

How much training is required to use this model? When I first looked at the model, it appeared a bit hard to grasp. It takes a little while to get used to the seven different components and their organization. But it was not long before I could remember what the components were and where to look for the specific information I wanted. The model does not require advanced theological or psychological training.

The data gathered in this assessment would also be of interest to professionals from other disciplines. The information about ultimate values, for example, would help other professional staff to understand factors in a patient's motivation for recovery or lack of it.

The model has also been developed so that the data generated for each patient can be entered into a computerized data base supporting a variety of analyses of patterns of spiritual needs in specific patient populations. The tool is simple enough that most components can be used in acute care settings where patients' acuity is high and length of stay is brief. But the data here is also extensive enough to support assessment and care planning for longer-term ministry, as in rehabilitation settings.

Because the model appears to be simple, there are several possible pitfalls that can be associated with using it. The first is the assumption that because one has completed the data gathering in the assessment, one has understood a person. There is a difference between having accurate information about someone and having an empathic understanding of that person. Tools such as this one can provide assistance with the former, but skill and training on the part of the caregiver are still required to achieve the latter. The second pitfall associated with objective models such as this is that they overlook the role of the relationship between the caregiver and care recipient and how this might or might not affect the data received. Further, this relationship can be an important factor in the effectiveness of the pastoral care plan. McSherry's model makes no mention of the relationship as a factor in implementing a care plan successfully. Finally, at its worst a model that emphasizes objective statistical information, as McSherry's does, can lead to the impressive statistical documentation of matters that are irrelevant or of secondary importance. Research needs to be conducted to test whether the key elements of spiritual life highlighted by this model are in fact relevant for understanding people's spiritual needs and providing pastoral care.

In summary, McSherry has provided a model for spiritual assessment that seeks to be concrete and objective. These features make the model very attractive because they enable a caregiver to conduct a practical and relatively comprehensive spiritual assessment quickly. The model encourages the patient to identify his or her own spiritual concerns and goals as well as spiritual resources. Because it employs a tacit evangelical Protestant conception of the spiritual life, the model will be most useful in assessment of persons who share that faith tradition. Some modification would be necessary for the model to be helpful with persons from other faith traditions, or those who were spiritual but did not identify themselves with a specific religious group.

The North American Nursing Diagnosis Association

Our colleagues in nursing have a longstanding interest in their patients' spiritual needs. This interest is evidenced in the substantial number of publications related to spiritual assessment that have appeared over the past fifteen to twenty years.[32] One of the most developed models for nursing spiritual assessment stems from the work of the North American Nursing Diagnosis Association (NANDA).[33]

Since its first conference in 1975, NANDA has developed a list of almost one hundred conditions that nurses are qualified to diagnose and treat. The conditions include biological problems (decreased cardiac output, constipation), psychological conditions (chronic low self-esteem, dysfunctional grieving), and interpersonal problems (social isolation, altered family processes).

The association defines a nursing diagnosis as "a clinical judgment about an individual, family, or community that is derived through a deliberate, systematic process of data collection and analysis. It provides the basis for prescriptions for definitive therapy for which the nurse is accountable. It is expressed concisely and includes the etiology of the condition when known."[34]

Each diagnosis has three parts: a label and definition; a statement of etiology (cause) or related factors; and a list of defining characteristics, specific observable signs, and symptoms associated with the diagnosis.[35] Nursing diagnoses are linked to the nursing process. The steps are similar to those outlined for the clinical ministry process and are used by a nurse to move from assessment to treatment.

At the third national conference of the association (1978), spiritual concerns, spiritual distress, and spiritual despair were approved as nursing diagnoses. At the fourth national conference (1980) these were combined into one category, spiritual distress.[36] Like any nursing diagnosis, the diagnosis of "spiritual distress (distress of the human spirit)" has three components: a definition, related factors, and defining characteristics.

Definition

Disruption in the life principle that pervades a person's entire being and that integrates and transcends one's biological and psychosocial nature.

Related factors [etiology]

Separation from religious and cultural ties

Challenged belief and value system (e.g., result of moral or ethical implications of therapy or result of intense suffering)

Defining characteristics

Expresses concern with meaning of life and death and/or belief system

Anger toward God (as defined by the person)

Questions meaning of suffering

Verbalizes inner conflict about beliefs

Verbalizes concern about relationship with deity

Questions meaning of own existence

Unable to choose or chooses not to participate in usual religious practices

Seeks spiritual assistance

Questions moral and ethical implications of therapeutic regimen

Displacement of anger toward religious representatives

Description of nightmares or sleep disturbances

Alteration in behavior or mood evidenced by anger, crying, withdrawal, preoccupation, anxiety, hostility, apathy, etc.

Regards illness as punishment

Does not experience that God is forgiving

Unable to accept self

Engages in self-blame

Denies responsibility for problems

Description of somatic complaints[37]

This definition of spiritual distress and its defining characteristics are the extent of the formal NANDA diagnosis. Secondary materials related to this and other nursing diagnoses have also been published. For example, Kim's *Pocket Guide to Nursing Diagnoses* includes a two-page prototype care plan for a homeless, alcoholic person diagnosed with spiritual distress. It includes patient goals, expected outcomes, and associated nursing interventions.[38]

Doenges and Moorhouse have also published a *Nurse's Pocket Guide* that, in addition to the NANDA diagnoses, provides a description of desired patient outcomes or evaluation criteria and specific nursing interventions. The specific outcomes and interventions listed are described as ones commonly found in adult patients in acute or long-term care settings and are provided to help the nurse formulate individual patient care plans. Desired patient outcomes for the diagnosis spiritual distress include "discusses beliefs/values about spiritual issues" and "verbalizes increased sense of self-esteem and hope for future." Examples of nursing interventions include "determine patient's religious/spiritual orientation," "establish environment that allows free expression of feelings and concerns," and "help patient find a reason for living."[39]

In 1983 Carpenito published a guide to the application of nursing diagnoses in clinical practice. While there have been important changes in the NANDA diagnoses since then, Carpenito's text has some material that pastoral caregivers may find interesting and helpful. Carpenito suggests five questions that could be added to a nursing psychosocial assessment to enable spiritual assessment. The questions are simple but thorough.

1. Is religion or God important to you?
   If answer is yes, to what religion do you belong? or in what do you believe?
   If answer is no, do you find a source of strength or meaning in another area?
2. What effect do you expect your illness (hospitalization) to have on your spiritual practices or beliefs?
3. Are there any religious books (statues, medals, services, places) that are especially important to you?
4. Do you have a special religious leader (priest, pastor, rabbi)?
5. How can I help you maintain your spiritual strength during this illness (hospitalization) (e.g., contact spiritual leader, provide privacy at special times, request reading materials)?[40]

Her discussion of spiritual distress has a nine-page table of the beliefs and practices of most major religious groups, related to health and illness. It includes non-Christian groups and is wonderfully useful. There is also a helpful list of principles and rationale for how and why nurses should be involved in spiritual care.[41] Carpenito, like Doenges and Moorhouse, also provides specific goals, outcome criteria, and interventions for two forms of spiritual distress, spiritual distress related to the inability to practice spiritual rituals and spiritual distress related to conflict with prescribed therapy.[42]

Nurses have applied their research skills to their work on spiritual diagnosis. An example is Judith Weatherall's validation study of the NANDA defining characteristics for spiritual distress. Weatherall reviewed thirty-four articles on spiritual issues written by nurses between 1959 and 1984. She also gathered case reports and care plans for thirteen patients who were diagnosed with spiritual distress by their nurses. She counted the "cues" in each article and case report and compared them to the twenty-two NANDA defining characteristics. She found strong support in both the literature and patient cases for only three of the NANDA characteristics: questions meaning of suffering, verbalizes concern about relationship with deity, and verbalizes inner conflict about beliefs. She also found support for two characteristics not in the NANDA list, hopelessness and relationships with other people. She concludes, "It is difficult to say that the characteristics are strongly supported and valid."[43]

Evaluation of the Model

Concept of Spirituality. The NANDA model has a very explicit definition of spirituality, "the life principle that pervades a person's entire being and that integrates and transcends one's biological and psychosocial nature." Sources for this definition, or related conceptualizations of human spirituality, are not provided. Ellerhorst-Ryan has characterized the definition as "a beginning . . . [but] vague and does not therefore lend itself easily to research,"[44] an observation that could probably be made about the majority of definitions of spirituality.

I have found no description of an underlying theological framework for this model. In fact the model appears to avoid a confessional foundation in order to be practically useful in assessing the spiritual distress of people from a wide variety of spiritual perspectives. Thus specific defining characteristics are worded to take into account a diversity of beliefs, such as "Anger toward God (as defined by the person)." The model seems to have a functional approach to defining spirituality.[45]

On closer look, however, it appears that the defining characteristics fall into two groups, one group that expresses the broad, functional view of spirituality (e.g., "Verbalizes inner conflict about beliefs") and another group that seems to grow out of views of the nature of God, of persons, or the God-person relationship that are more particular to the Christian faith tradition (e.g., "Does not experience that God is forgiving," or "Regards illness as punishment"). An item such as the former would not be useful in assessing the spiritual distress of a spiritual but nontheistic believer.

The defining characteristics suggest a multidimensional view of spirituality, directing attention to beliefs, values, rituals, and other practices. The related factors and defining characteristics also give some attention to relationships and religious and cultural ties. The concept of spirituality in the model focuses strongly on the literal construction of the patient's verbal statements, but attention to alteration in moods and behavior, and to displacement of anger toward religious representatives, implies some ability to embrace a dynamic view of spirituality. The model has no evidence of a developmental view of spirituality.

The model's basic definition of spirituality expresses a holistic view, with spirituality pervading and integrating other dimensions of life. The view that illness or health in one dimension of life, such as the spiritual, has an impact on illness or health in other dimensions has long been an important principle in nursing. Carpenito gives expression to it in the third principle she identifies, "The nature of the spiritual care an individual receives may directly affect the speed and quality of his [or her] recovery from illness."[46] What direction can interaction between the dimensions of life take, according to the model? Clearly biological problems, intense suffering, for example, can contribute to spiritual distress. The model is less clear about how mental illness or cultural traditions might alter spiritual well-being and express themselves in some of its defining characteristics.

For the most part the model does a good job of maintaining a distinct view of the spiritual dimension of life, a difficult task for most functional views of spirituality. However, it is difficult to see the distinction between the spiritual and the psychosocial in some of the defining characteristics, such as alteration in mood, nightmares, self-blame, and somatic complaints. Not surprisingly, Weatherall's study suggests that these are some of the defining characteristics with the least support in the literature and case reports she reviewed.

Norms and Authority. The formal description of the model contains no explicit discussion of the issues of norms or values and power or authority in the process of diagnosis.

Norms and values about spiritual health are easiest to discern in the secondary literature, such as the expected outcomes of spiritual care listed by Doenges and Moorhouse ("verbalizes increased sense of self-esteem and hope for future," "demonstrates ability to help self/participate in care")[47] and in the goals and expected outcomes in the prototype care plan in Kim ("achieves high score on Spiritual Well-Being Index of Paloutzian and Ellison," "articulates and is comfortable with belief system").[48] This literature also points out the importance of the nurse's being aware of her own religious perspectives and not imposing them on the patients she is caring for, "Be aware of the caregiver's belief system. It is still possible to be helpful to patient while remaining neutral."[49]

The model assumes a situation of spiritual need or distress. It has no explicit discussion of the role of the parties in the spiritual assessment process. Some of the literature indicates an awareness of the need to be attentive to the patient's definition of his or her spiritual needs and goals. "Use therapeutic communication skills of reflection, Active Listening, etc., to help patient find own solutions to concerns."[50]

Assessment Context and Process. The model was obviously developed for use in various health-related contexts. The formal description of the model assumes a context of distress, of separation from normal cultural or religious roots, or of challenged beliefs. This assumption is carried over in the specific defining characteristics, which also assume distress.

In this light the model doesn't seem well suited for contexts in which distress is absent, contexts focusing more on normal spiritual growth or development.[51] But actually the assumption of distress is so broadly conceived that the model seems to be potentially useful in a wide variety of contexts, not just medical hospitals or clinics, but even in parishes or schools, where persons are not immune to episodes of spiritual trial and distress.

I have found no discussion of whether the model can be used with children or persons whose cognitive functioning is impaired by organic or mental illness, although some of the defining characteristics seem to lend themselves well to this broader application. Some characteristics would be less useful with these groups, such as "Expresses concern with the meaning of life and death."

Although the model was developed for use by nurses, nothing in its formal description would prevent other pastoral care providers from making fruitful use of it. In fact the model's link to the nursing process, with its clear description of the steps of clinical reasoning and therapeutic action, makes it a useful tool to enhance the clarity of our thinking about our spiritual assessment, care plans, and interventions.

The list of defining characteristics appears to be a major strength of the model. At a number of points they bear remarkable similarity to the ten specific spiritual concerns employed by McSherry (e.g., anger toward God, inner conflict about beliefs, moral and ethical nature of medical plan, suffering/theodicy). Their specificity directs the caregiver's attention to explicit expressions of spiritual distress. The model is less helpful in directing attention to signs of spiritual ill health that may not be causing distress to the patient, such as substance abuse. Like any list, this one is not exhaustive.

A central strength of this model is its practicality. The model enables a caregiver to attend quickly to areas of spiritual pain and to begin to plan ways to address them. Its list of the possible areas of spiritual distress covers areas of concern that I frequently encounter in my clinical practice. The inclusion of the related factors, etiology, also adds to the practicality of the model. It quickly focuses attention on possible causes of spiritual distress that could be addressed in specific interventions.

The model's defining characteristics, while quite specific and concrete, still leave room for interpretation and misinterpretation. If a patient says, "Why doesn't God listen to my prayers?" is that evidence of "concern about relationship with deity" or "anger toward God"? Fortunately it does not appear that such specific interpretations are necessary. Either characteristic is acceptable, and the patient's remark is seen as evidence of spiritual distress, which the caregiver can now attend to. In general the model does seem generous in its definition of what might constitute distress, and we might expect few false negative assessments.

Are there levels of spiritual distress? The model doesn't directly address this question. How then does the caregiver know whether the distress is mild or profound? Is it by number of defining characteristics observed, or some other measure? How would assessing the level of distress affect the care plan? This matter appears to require the clinical judgment of the caregiver.

The caregiver's judgment or interpretation also appears to be important in making the transition from data gathering to data interpretation (diagnosis) to care plan. The specific expected outcomes and interventions in the secondary literature provide appealing and helpful specific suggestions, but they really do not replace clinical judgment.

In considering this model's goals and interventions, one gets an impression of naïveté. In Kim's prototypical case of the homeless alcoholic, one of the goals is "develop support system with friends/church members."[52] We all might hope that the patient would be ready for help with previous patterns of social isolation and difficulty with interpersonal relations, but it is quite likely that for such a patient these are longstanding problems. Their resolution requires much more effort than simply writing the goals did. Doenges and Moorhouse's intervention, "help patient find a reason for living,"[53] is similar. Most of the suggested interventions and expected outcomes imply that things could be made better and in a relatively brief period of time. In my hospital experience, ministry usually focuses on sustaining a person against further erosion in spiritual well-being in the face of continuing or worsening health problems. Thus, the goal for a homeless alcoholic would be effective use of support offered by health care professionals in the hospital environment. Likewise, helping a patient find a reason for living would be translated into helping the patient accept medical treatment as a way to better health. Nurses can certainly be as effective in this ministry as chaplains and pastors. It is unfortunate that this is not given greater recognition and legitimation in the literature.

The literature does give attention to those interventions that have been central in the history of pastoral care: a trusting relationship of unconditional acceptance and the establishment of an environment that allows free expression of feelings and concerns.[54]

The link to ministry generally implied in this model is the ministry of the nurse. It is assumed that the nurse is able to make a spiritual assessment and to provide the spiritual care that addresses his or her patient's spiritual distress. At the same time, the suggested interventions include referral to spiritual leaders and religious counselors for further assistance.[55]

The model appears to be quite user friendly. The specificity of the defining characteristics imply that little training is required to conduct the data gathering phase of the assessment. As already noted, more training and experience would be required to interpret the data obtained and to formulate an effective care plan.

This model makes it easy to communicate to other professionals and to the patient and family the data that provides the basis for an assessment of spiritual distress. One of the model's virtues is the behaviorally specific and "experience-near" nature of the defining characteristics.

Other models with similar levels of concreteness and simplicity (McSherry comes to mind) rely on a structured or semi-structured interview for data gathering. While Carpenito provides a mini-structured interview to guide data gathering, the formal model does not include or suggest a structured interview. Rather assessment could proceed in a more informal conversational mode, as in traditional pastoral care. Observations made during the interview could later be organized and reported in light of the model's defining characteristics. The defining characteristics, however, also lend themselves to use as a checklist, which would make an effective baseline measure of spiritual distress against which progress or lack of it could be measured. Such a tool would be useful in quality assurance programs and in research about spiritual care.

In summary, the NANDA model for spiritual assessment, while developed for nurses, could be a useful tool for other pastoral caregivers as well. Using the term *spiritual distress*, the model also focuses on religious distress caused by separation from accustomed practices, conflict between beliefs and recommended therapy, and doubts created by intense suffering. The model is multidimensional, considering beliefs, practices, and key relationships. The defining characteristics in the model are very specific and can be useful in both clinical practice and research.

NOTES

1. A review of twenty-six models of spiritual assessment, using the guidelines from chap. 6, is available in George Fitchett, *Spiritual Assessment in Pastoral Care: A Guide to Selected Resources* (Decatur, Ga.: Journal of Pastoral Care Publications, forthcoming).

2. Pruyser describes his guidelines as "provisional" (*The Minister as Diagnostician*, 80). When he learned of Malony's use of the guidelines in the Religious Status Interview, he wrote to Malony expressing his displeasure. See Malony, "Critical Assessment," 3.

Published models based on Pruyser's "Guidelines," include Malony, ibid.; Weiss, "Pastoral Care Planning"; Greg Stoddard and Jean Burns-Haney, "Developing an Integrated Approach to Spiritual Assessment: One Department's Experience," *The Care Giver Journal* 7, 1 (1990): 63–86; Sackett, "Seven Dimensions"; and Albert Blomquist, "Teaching Jail Inmates to Diagnose Their Religious Experiences," *Journal of Pastoral Care* 38, 1 (March 1984): 17–28.

I have seen several unpublished models for spiritual assessment that also employ Pruyser's seven categories. David Stancil at the Southern Baptist Theological Seminary, Louisville, Kentucky, has used them in developing the "Pastoral Counseling

Inventory," a tool designed to measure changes in the spiritual aspect of life as a result of psychotherapy.

3. *The Minister as Diagnostician*, 20.

4. Ibid., 27.

5. Ibid., 55.

6. Ibid., 83.

7. Ibid., 67.

8. Ibid., 68.

9. Fowler, *Stages of Faith;* Westerhoff, *Will Our Children Have Faith?*

10. Pruyser, *The Minister as Diagnostician*, 64.

11. Ibid., p. 51.

12. For examples see ibid., 67, 69, 72, 86.

13. See ibid., 84, for an indication that Pruyser recognizes that the diagnostic perspectives of different professions often rely on concepts taken from another profession.

14. Ibid., 28.

15. Ibid., 90.

16. Ibid.

17. This analysis is not meant to argue that Pruyser was not capable of more nuanced appreciation of these issues. His work *The Play of the Imagination: Toward a Psychoanalysis of Culture* (New York: International Universities Press, 1983), gives evidence that he was. He did not apply that more sophisticated appreciation of these issues to this book.

18. *The Minister as Diagnostician*, 80–81.

19. Ibid., 85–86.

20. Ibid., 95–96, emphasis in the original.

21. Ibid., 95.

22. Elisabeth McSherry, "The Modernization of Chaplaincy," *Care Giver* 4, 1 (August 1987): 1.

23. For further discussion of these points see McSherry, "Modernization"; idem, "The Need and Appropriateness of Measurement and Research in Chaplaincy: Its Criticalness for Patient Care and Chaplain Department Survival Post-1987," *Journal of Health Care Chaplaincy* 1, 1 (Fall/Winter 1987): 3–41; idem, "The Crisis in Health Care: Pastoral Care in the DRG World," *Proceedings of the 1986 ACPE Conference, Crisis: Danger and Opportunity,* (Atlanta, Ga., October 1986), 28–50; McSherry and William A. Nelson, "The DRG Era: A Major Opportunity for Increased Pastoral Care Impact or a Crisis for Survival," *Journal of Pastoral Care* 41, 3 (September 1987): 201–11; and McSherry, Kratz, and Nelson, "Pastoral Care Departments."

24. The SPA can be found in McSherry, Kratz, and Nelson, "Pastoral Care Departments."Both the SPA and the SSI were included, under separate cover, with the issue of the *Care Giver* 4, 1, (August 1987) devoted to McSherry's presentations at the College of Chaplains annual meeting in March 1987. An updated version of the Clinical Assessment Data Card can be found in Steven R. Salisbury, Megan R. Ciulla, and Elisabeth McSherry, "Clinical Management Reporting and Objective Diagnostic Instruments for Spiritual Assessment in Spinal Cord Injury Patients," *Journal of Health Care Chaplaincy* 2, 2 (1989): 35–64.

25. A description of the original scale can be found in Thomas H. Holmes and Richard H. Rahe, "The Social Re-adjustment Rating Scale," *Journal of Psychosomatic Research* 11 (1967): 213–18. A copy of the scale may also be found in Clinebell, *Basic Types,* 189.

26. McSherry refers to this as "Kasl's Religiosity Index" in both the SPA and her 1986 *HCM Review* article. Her citation of the authors of the original research article in that paper is incorrect. The authors listed on the article are Zuckerman, Diana M., S. Kasl, and A. Ostfeld.

27. See Milton Rokeach, *The Nature of Human Values* (New York: The Free Press, 1973), and William McCready and Andrew K. Greeley, *The Ultimate Values of Americans* (Beverly Hills: Sage Publications, 1975).

28. McSherry, SSI, 1.

29. Ibid.

30. Salisbury et al., "Clinical Management Reporting."

31. McSherry, SSI, 1.

32. For example see Sharon Fish and Judith Allen Shelley, *Spiritual Care: The Nurse's Role* (Downers Grove, Ill.: InterVarsity Press, 1978), and Verna Benner Carson, ed., *Spiritual Dimensions of Nursing Practice* (Philadelphia: W. B. Saunders, 1989).

33. The association's address is NANDA, St. Louis University School of Nursing, 3525 Caroline Avenue, St. Louis, MO 63014.

34. Kim, McFarland, and McLane, *Pocket Guide to Nursing Diagnosis*, 3d ed. (St. Louis: C. V. Mosby, 1989), xi.

35. Kim et al., *Pocket Guide*, 1984, 4–5.

36. Jan Ellerhorst-Ryan, "Selecting an Instrument to Measure Spiritual Distress," *Oncology Nursing Forum* 12, 2 (March/April 1985): 93.

37. Kim et al., *Pocket Guide*, 1989, 62–63.

38. Ibid., 268–69.

39. Marilynn E. Doenges and Mary Frances Moorhouse, *Nurse's Pocket Guide: Nursing Diagnoses with Interventions*, 2d ed. (Philadelphia: F. A. Davis, 1988), 351–53.

40. Carpenito, *Nursing Diagnosis*, 452.

41. For a further discussion of nurses' reluctance to identify spiritual care as an aspect of their role, see Sandra L. Granstrom, "Spiritual Nursing Care for Oncology Patients," *Topics in Clinical Nursing*, April 1985, 39–45.

42. Carpenito, *Nursing Diagnosis*, 452–66.

43. Judith D. Weatherall, "Validation of the Nursing Diagnosis Spiritual Distress" (Master's thesis, University of Illinois, Chicago, 1985), 12.

44. Ellerhorst-Ryan, "Selecting an Instrument," 93.

45. Carpenito is explicit in stating this as her first principle: "All people have a spiritual dimension, whether or not they participate in formal religious practices" (*Nursing Diagnosis*, 452).

46. Ibid.

44. Doenges and Moorhouse, *Nurse's Pocket Guide*, 351.

48. Kim et al., *Pocket Guide*, 1989, 268–69.

49. Doenges and Moorhouse, *Nurse's Pocket Guide*, 352. See also Carpenito, *Nursing Diagnosis*, 452.

50. Doenges and Moorhouse, *Nurse's Pocket Guide*, 353.

51. See Westberg's Whole Person Health Inventory for an alternative model that is more appropriate for a wellness context. Granger Westberg, *The Parish Nurse* (Minneapolis: Augsburg, 1990), 85–90.

52. Kim et al., *Pocket Guide*, 1989, 269.

53. Doenges and Moorhouse, *Nurse's Pocket Guide*, 353.

54. Ibid., 352.

55. Ibid., 353, and Carpenito, *Nursing Diagnosis*, 463, 465–66.

Chapter 8

THE SPIRIT
OF ASSESSMENT

Pastoral care and counseling in the second half of this century has placed a strong emphasis on the relationship between the caregiver and care recipient. There has also been an emphasis on the person of the caregiver, on becoming aware of our strengths and weaknesses so that we are optimally available to enter into healing and caring relationships with others. In trying to provide tools to assist caregivers with the work of spiritual assessment, I do not mean to replace or diminish the emphasis on the caring relationship or the person of the caregiver. They are topics that deserve our continued attention.

In this conclusion I describe some of the particular demands an interest in spiritual assessment makes on the person of the caregiver. I also share some thoughts about the continuing importance of the relationship in pastoral care. Finally, I mention some of my hopes for the directions that further work on spiritual assessment might take.

The work of spiritual assessment makes four demands on the person of the caregiver. The first demand is for modesty. Complex models for spiritual assessment tempt us to assume that if we use the model diligently, we will surely have an accurate picture of the spiritual life of the person we are caring for. After all, the complexity of models such as the 7 × 7 model or Fowler's theory of faith development is a result of an effort to have the most encompassing conceptualization of spirituality possible. Learning to use these models is often a demanding task. The caregiver who masters one or more of the models understandably takes some pride in that accomplishment and places confidence in the spiritual assessments that result.

However, the complexity of the material we are dealing with, the spiritual dimension of life as it relates to a holistic understanding of the person, requires that we treat our models with modesty. Maria Harris quotes a story about two famous astronomers that reminds me of this. "Consider Johannes Kepler, imagine him on a hill watching the dawn. With him is Tycho Brahe. Kepler regarded the sun as fixed. It was the earth that moved. But Tycho followed Ptolemy and Aristotle in this much at least: the earth was fixed and all other celestial bodies moved around it. Question: Do Kepler and Tycho see the same thing in the east at dawn"?[1]

Our models for spiritual assessment, based on our theories about the spiritual aspect of life, will direct our attention to some phenomena and cause us to overlook others. We do our best to develop models that we believe focus on the phenomena that are important for spiritual assessment in pastoral care. Yet there is surely room for improvement and cause for us to be modest in our approach toward our models and the spiritual assessments we develop with them.

The second demand that spiritual assessment makes on the caregiver is for playfulness. In his book *In Praise of Play*, Robert Neale describes play as activity that is not undertaken in order to resolve conflict.[2] Work, the opposite of play, is activity with which we try to resolve conflict. These definitions reflect experiences I have had and have seen in others, such as when I am working too hard at trying to relax, or when my work is a source of delight, as it can be in spiritual assessment.

From this perspective, a playful approach to spiritual assessment will naturally be characterized by the modesty I just mentioned. A playful approach to spiritual assessment may help us avoid the rigidity and abuse that can accompany the use of models of pastoral diagnosis if we are not careful.

The third demand that spiritual assessment places on the caregiver is for continued personal self-awareness. This is not a new concern and has been an important emphasis of our field for quite a while. However, the use of spiritual assessment tools could tempt us to believe we have an objective basis for our pastoral care plans that remove the possibility of personal bias or distortion. Our models for spiritual assessment cannot do that for us. As we saw in the review of the different models in the previous two chapters, they provide assistance primarily in more systematic information gathering. The work of interpreting that information and developing a care plan based on the information still rests to a great extent on the knowledge and judgment of the caregiver. Thus the possibility of personal biases or needs distorting our spiritual assessments is not ended, and caregivers need to continue to grow in self-awareness.

The fourth demand that spiritual assessment places on the caregiver is for cultural self-awareness. As the review of models indicated, every approach to spiritual assessment embodies, either explicitly or implicitly, a set of norms against which a person is being evaluated. As caregivers we need to supplement our work on personal self-awareness with attention to the ways in which our place in our culture shapes us. Our race, our class, and our gender are forceful factors shaping our self-understanding and the norms against which we judge others. We must guard against using spiritual assessment tools to impose those norms on others for whom they are inappropriate. Our goal need not be to free ourselves of all biases but rather through consciousness raising to become aware of our biases. This will help us be alert to situations where we might be more likely to need help in making an assessment. In those situations we might seek the consultation of another person or ask the person with whom we are working to provide further clarification.

How would you evaluate my ability to respond to these four demands, to be modest, playful, and personally and culturally self-aware? I would say that modesty was evident in my work with Ethel. As the case reveals, she did not really share my assessment of her needs or my care plan. My modesty about my assessment was expressed as I respected her choices yet continued our relationship.

What about my playfulness? I must confess my sense that my participation in developing the 7 × 7 model was marked by work more than play. I could not bear the thought of a model for spiritual assessment that omitted any important aspect of human existence. Developing the model was a place where I expressed my conflicts about the need for control and order over life. Working on the model with colleagues I respected helped me maintain some perspective. Testing the model with other colleagues and students also helped. Hopefully this introduction to the model has not been too much work for you, and you will be able to employ it in your ministry in creative and playful manner.

Do you see any blind spots in my personal self-awareness in the cases I reported or my assessment of them? I hope that I have enough knowledge of myself so that I did not inappropriately project my issues onto Ethel or into my assessment of Mrs. Gabatino or Bob. Although I did not mention it in the case reports, I am aware of some similarities between issues in my life and those that these people were dealing with. Matters relating to self-worth and handling conflict with those I am close to are examples in Ethel's case. I hope that my assessment of Ethel and my care for her were not unduly biased by this.

What do the cases and the other material in this book say about my cultural self-awareness, about the way in which the place I occupy in our culture shapes what I see around me? I have tried to be sensitive to this issue. In fact we included an assessment of race, culture, and ethnicity and of societal issues in the 7 × 7 model because we think these issues are important.

An increased interest in spiritual assessment should complement, not displace, our emphasis on the caregiver's strengths and weaknesses, biases and motives. It also should complement the emphasis we have placed on the pastoral relationship. I have tried to highlight this by including an examination of the ways different spiritual assessment models address the issue of authority between the parties in the assessment process. But beyond that, more precise or complex spiritual assessments by themselves do not provide comfort, healing, or spiritual growth. They must be translated into care plans, and those plans must be expressed in caring relationships. The emphasis we as caregivers have placed on being present to the person we are caring for, on providing faithful companionship to the person, is not changed by our additional interest in spiritual assessment.

I think the work of Chaplain Helen with Mrs. Gabatino is a good illustration of this. In her first visit with Mrs. Gabatino she heard something that caught her attention. She heard Minnie Gabatino's anxiety about her current hospitalization and the grief over her child's death. The chaplain's care for Minnie led her to go back to see her later that day, and when the subject of her child's death came up again, to say to her, "Tell me what her name was." This kind of care, this willingness to hear the sad and painful stories people need to tell, this willingness to be faithfully present as people wait, not knowing what the future holds—this is still the central way our spiritual assessments are translated into ministry.

I want to conclude with some suggestions about future work with spiritual assessment. First, I hope that our efforts to be more intentional about spiritual assessment in our ministry will be accompanied by more published case reports of pastoral care. We need this kind of information so that we can explore the issues further: decisions about what model of assessment we used, the way we gathered information to make our assessment, the difference the assessment made in our care plan and ministry, and whether the results of the care were as we had expected. There is much that we need to learn in each of these areas, and the best way for us to do this will be to share extensive case reports with one another.

Second, I hope that in the future we will increase the research we do related to spiritual assessment. One of the factors that has contributed to the increased interest in spiritual assessment in health care-related ministries has been pressure to document what pastoral care contributes to a patient's hospital stay. In order to describe the changes that result from pastoral care, we need to be able to describe what things were like before pastoral care was provided. Some research might choose to study the effect of pastoral care with measures such as shorter lengths of stay in the hospital or less need for pain medication. Other research will require a baseline spiritual assessment for comparison of a patient's spiritual needs after pastoral care. I hope that the future will see research that tests the assumptions in our spiritual assessment models, and research that employs spiritual assessment to study the results of our pastoral care.

Finally, I hope that future work in spiritual assessment will help us find a meaningful language for spirituality. As I discussed in chapter 7, Pruyser failed to appreciate that part of the reason pastors became so interested in the language of psychology in the middle of this century was that they had no other language with which to speak meaningfully of the spiritual dimension of life in a dynamic way. Developments in philosophy, science, and especially psychology called into question the literal truth of traditional religious language. A greater pluralism in our communities and the questioning of traditional authority also challenged the relevance of religious language that was identified with any narrow confessional tradition. In the face of these challenges no meaningful language of spirituality was available, and pastors turned to the language of psychology. I hope that as we continue our work on spiritual assessment we will find a convincing and helpful way to speak of and to the spiritual resources, struggles, and longings of those we minister to. I hope that we can find a language that combines the rich resources of our various religious traditions with the insights of modern psychology and speaks convincingly to people from a variety of traditional and nontraditional faith perspectives in order to minister to the whole person.

NOTES

1. Norwood Hansen, *Patterns of Discovery* (Cambridge, Mass.: Cambridge University Press, 1958), 5. Quoted by Maria Harris, "Completion and Faith Development," in Dykstra and Parks, eds., *Faith Development*, 119.
2. See Robert E. Neale, *In Praise of Play: Toward a Psychology of Religion* (New York: Harper & Row, 1969).

CPSIA information can be obtained
at www.ICGtesting.com
Printed in the USA
BVOW08s1701130717

489196BV00007B/138/P

9 780788 099403